Journey to Freedom

Journey to Freedom

A young boy's mission to reclaim the
life he lost during the Holocaust

This book begins where *My Brother's Voice* ended.

Author:
STEPHEN PISTA NASSER

Editor:
LINDA SCHWANDT

ISBN: 1514209039
ISBN 13: 9781514209035
Library of Congress Control Number: 2015914027
CreateSpace Independent Publishing Platform
North Charleston, South Carolina

Preface

My *Brother's Voice* ended as I bid a sad farewell to Vera, the girl I wished to spend my life with, and boarded a train at the Western Railway Station in Budapest.

I began my new adventure with hope and the expectation that Vera and I would soon be together again.

As I traveled toward an unknown future, I did so with a heavy heart, yet with an eagerness to experience life, urged on by the promise I had made to my brother, Andris. A promise to share my diary and inform people of the horror of the Holocaust so that history's most vicious genocide could never happen again. My journey to Canada via Paris, London, and with

Pista in 1948 said goodbye to Vera

a possibility of ending up in the U.S.A. It was highlighted when I finally beheld the symbol of freedom, the Statue of Liberty.

That was a lifetime ago. It was 1948 and I was a teenager. The years have flown by, and I realize how swiftly the time has passed as I write the rest of my story. Why such a long wait you may wonder? I was spending my life building a family and making sure that every day I was keeping my word to my brother, Andris. I filled my days with love while teaching others to do the same.

I did publish our story and spoke with audiences in many countries on over 1000 occasions. To my surprise, I had countless requests from readers and lecture attendees to share with them the rest of my story. As you venture through these pages, they will transport you on a remarkable journey.

Stephen "Pista" Nasser

"Not Yet, Pista"

First Andris, then Pista, brothers
Were born onto the sea of life,
To a family of loving parents,
Were protected from harm and strife.

They sailed through happy childhood
Educated side by side.
Andris was Pista's hero
Was never let out of his sight.

As they grew up year by year
Created a tight bond to last
Never to be broken
By any storm Evil can cast.

As clouds of despair darkened the sky,
The brothers found strength and trust
In each other's company
Even the rough seas, could not bust.

Growing up became a challenge
As the Nazis stormed in their lives,
Tossed them apart from the ones they loved
And took their family, never to be found alive.

At a tender age, the orphans were deported
To Auschwitz Death Camp
Beaten, starved, and degraded,
Their love gave them inner strength.

Loosing strength and lots of weight
Their survival began to quickly wane.
Pista wrote his diary
Assured his hope would never fade.

Andris weakened as time marched by
Tossed around within the storm.
Pista made a promise to his brother
He would never be forlorn.

Andris passed in Pista's arms,
The Nazis succeeded in killing the brother
But failed to break their bond
And their love for one another.

The fury of the storm has passed,
Pista kept his promise to his brother
He shared his diary and spread the word
As they had agreed one to the other.

Years gone by,
Memories are faded,
But Andris and Pista's bond
Will never be degraded.

As unconscious Pista was liberated,
He thought he saw his brother in heaven.
He called out, "I want to be with you!"
Andris replied, "Not Yet, Pista! You have time given."

Stephen "Pista" Nasser

One

TRAIN TO PARIS

I was sitting on the speeding train, unaware of the outside world. My mind was tortured, overrun with memories. I had my eyes closed; focusing on the last moment I shared with Vera when the image changed into Andris. *"You made the right decision, for both of you!"* It some-what eased my mind. Andris and I were separated, but our bond was stronger than life. He was there for me when I needed him. Vera was my gift from above; she made up for some of my loss. Every time I awoke, she was there for me. From fondness grew love, and I was filled with happiness. We were deeply in love and decided to get married in freedom and start a family. She knew I would not settle for our children to be raised under the post- Nazi Communism that we were forced to endure. My dad did not have a chance to save us, but history taught me a hard lesson, **Never Again**. I knew deep in my heart, I had made the right decision at my tender age of 16.

The sharp whistle of the train brought me back to reality. I gazed through the window as the landscape changed; the grazing cows and villages slipped by, and the sun peeked through some fluffy clouds. I'm on the "Freedom Train" I thought. After visiting the dining car I felt better, eager to take on the world single-handed.

Out of my train compartment, standing in the hallway, I was staring through the open window watching the powerful steam engine transporting me to my new life ahead. The white-grayish smoke swept in our direction as the train was slowing to go around a curve. The smoke made my eyes tear, as I raised the window. Not too far from me to the right there was a middle-aged gentleman doing the same thing. As we both stepped back rubbing our eyes, simultaneously we smiled at each other. He commented in American English, "I think we both got the message," at least I thought that was what he meant. My English and German were weak, but I managed to communicate, aided by hand gestures. His face looked somehow familiar to me. He invited me to join him for lunch. During our conversation, I tried to ask him where he lived, switching from English to German, and unintentionally, slipping in some Hungarian words. He was amused as I did not give up trying to communicate. I told him that I thought I had seen him somewhere before. He assured me that personally he had never been in Budapest. We had a good time as we approached Switzerland.

At each border crossing we had to present our passports to the custom officers who boarded the train. My new friend prepared to get off at the next stop, but before he departed he gave me a big, brotherly hug. My eyes must have teared, as I remembered Andris. He motioned to me to go to the window and open it, and I waved good-bye to him. I watched him as he headed for a couple of Swiss candy machines and returned to my open window, and handed me several bars of Swiss Chocolate. I was overwhelmed. We shook hands as I thanked him in English, German and Hungarian. He sported a big smile as the train pulled out. We kept on waving until we could not see each other. (A year or so later in Canada I saw him again. A motion picture, *Sword in the Desert* was playing, starring Dana Andrews. I'm sure he was the nice gentleman. Earlier in Hungary, Vera and I had seen some of his pictures and he had a very memorable profile.)

The long train ride allowed me plenty of time to organize my thoughts. I had my memories-lots of mental and physical scars, the burden of the past, and the promise of the future. The past is history, no one can change it. I'm part of the future, and I will not let down Andris. I had promised him that I would share my diary with the public. I have not worked on my diary since I re-wrote it in the hospital, so it was still in a few notebooks scribbled in Hungarian. I really was not up to do much with it at this time. I felt Uncle Charles should not learn the terrible secret I was hiding in those pages; the truth of how his beloved wife, Bozsi and his little son, Peter were murdered by the Nazi bullies. I made a commitment to myself to keep his family's murders a secret until he passes away. It was not an easy task to keep the story hidden for so many years. My uncle was healthy and enjoyed his life with his second wife Ilonka. She was perfect for him, as she had also lost her husband to the Nazis.

By the time I arrived at the Montparnasse Station in Paris, a prearranged representative from The Jewish Congress picked me up and took me to an old hotel located on Rue Rassin. I didn't care about beauty or location, I was in Paris!! Happy and exhausted, I dragged the steamer luggage up to the third floor. I didn't even unpack; I just passed out on the bed.

After a great night's sleep, I was awakened by my growling stomach. I showered, unpacked some clothing, and then ran down the staircase, hopping two steps at a time. As I opened the entry door, I took a deep breath of the Parisian air, filled with freedom and excitement. I could not wait to roam the streets, and grab something to eat in a local, small coffee house. I had some Franks in my pocket, given to me by my friendly social worker on arrival, but I was too thrifty to spend my money so quickly. I visited the famous Champs Elyse, the Eiffel Tower, and the Louvre, hopping on buses and taking the Paris subway.

I thought, only two short years ago, I was boarding trains, without paying or having papers to identify myself, heading back from hell to my home in Budapest. It was a challenge but I made it. Today it was a different situation in a strange city.. I had Vera on my mind, and I was determined to have her with me, sometime in the future, as husband and wife, discovering places unknown to us. Just the thought of her warmed my heart. I also managed to give a smile to my beloved brother, Andris. I was full of vigor and determination. There is no one who can stop me. I had no problems, only challenges. I felt Life was beautiful.

Just a few days later, I was transported by the Jewish Agency to a facility outside Versailles, located in a small community, called Jouy-en-Josas. There I joined some other Hungarian orphans. The dozen or so fellow comrades welcomed me, and asked lots of questions about traveling alone from Budapest to Paris. There was Gyuri, and his younger brother, and then Zsuzsi, Jutka, Heidy, Imre, Marika, Laci, Pali, Marta, Eva, and the Moses sisters, Kitty and Boci. To qualify for this "Freedom" transport, we had to be less than 17 years of age and single individuals. Imre and Heidy looked somewhat older, and they traveled as cousins. We discovered later they were a married couple. To our delight we also learned that Imre shaved his hairy legs to avoid suspicion, and, of course, they had false documents.

During the weeks we spent together, I could not hide my deep affection for Vera.

There were some flirtations between the youngsters, but I was never part of this, as I kept busy writing to Vera. Of course the "Kissing Cousins", Heidy and Imre, were doing their own thing. We all went on hikes and watched movies, even though we barely understood the language. This lack of understanding gave us lots of time together to discuss the meanings of the films we had just seen. We were bogged down waiting to get the necessary papers and tickets to go to England, so we could get to the final destination, Canada. The famous personality, Leon Blume, a staunch Communist, was the head of the shelter where we were. He was helped by his son, Joe Torres, who did a good job of keeping us in control. We pestered him a lot, as we were getting impatient, wondering when we would receive our travel documents.

The long awaited day finally arrived! I had mailed a letter to Vera, bringing her up to date with my travel plans. We boarded our transportation to take us to the train station in Paris. Once again we were aboard and our luggage was secured. For me it was a glorious day, a new challenge, a step closer to freedom, and Canada, our final destination!

For a second, I closed my eyes and shared some thoughts with Andris.

South Hampton to Canada

Arriving in England, I got what I expected, fog and mist. The Jewish Agency had everything under control. Without their help, I would not be where I am today. We got settled in a small hotel; it wasn't the Hilton, but to me, it was Paradise. We had a few days on our own, so we did some sightseeing, but could enjoy only as much as the fog allowed us: The Tower Bridge, Parliament, and Piccadilly Circus. We were all prepared to leave the following morning having packed for our ocean journey. We had a traditional English breakfast: crumpets, butter and jam, tea and coffee. I did not touch the herring as fish is not my favorite food. Even years ago, when I went fishing with Andris, we had an agreement. I baited the hook, and slid the worm on it, but Andris removed those slimy, stinking fish from the hook. Of course mother fried them, and I pretended that I was conveniently not hungry enough to eat much of the fried fish. But at least they were fried; these smelly herrings looked raw to me. I did not have to pretend now, to please anyone. I enjoyed my freedom, my freedom of choice and thoughts.

I had lost my family, and at the same time my youthful years with it. None of that could ever be recovered. I had almost lost my life. I had been transformed from a young boy, to maturity. Like they say, "Sink or swim." I just challenged the world to try and stop me now, and it would fail. With the confidence of having Andris looking over me, I knew I would keep my promise to him, and meet any future challenges. That was me, "Pista", no more a little boy.

We were transported to South Hampton. Standing on the dock, we could not believe our eyes, as our jaws dropped in amazement. There was a huge ocean liner, *The Aquitania*, black and gleaming white, with a multiple-storied deck, a giant topped with four huge red chimneys. She was a beauty!

I was really excited to board my "Ship to Freedom" and sail toward a new world.

The Jewish Congress had given us $3.00 spending money, and I felt rich. My wallet was not bulging, but my spirits were sky high. I've learned the hard way that if you have a good attitude the world is in your palm, and I practiced what I preached. Of course we were not in first class. Who cared? I had no fancy clothes to wear, but in my mind I was richer then Rockefeller and I was floating on cloud nine. We shared cabins, and we each had a bunk bed. But instead of straw for a mattress like back in the Concentration Camps, we had white sheets and fluffy pillows. We could

The ship Aquitania, brought Stephen and several orphans to Halifax, Canada.

They all signed the card.

fall asleep in comfort, without nightmares haunting us. Life was great, and I think most of us fully appreciated the reality. Adjusting to daily life was a pleasurable accomplishment.

In the morning our first breakfast was an adventure. All of us orphans and just a few of us Holocaust survivors sat around this huge, oblong table with white tablecloths, napkins, and silverware, and china dishes. Waiters were serving us hot coffee, tea, or milk, whatever we fancied, warm breakfast rolls, butter and jam, ham and eggs if we chose. In the middle of the table there was a large bowl filled some sort of flakes. I didn't feel like eating that funny kind of potato chip early in the morning. Then we looked at a table beside us, and saw people taking some of the chips in their empty bowls and putting sugar and milk on top. I thought they were savages—cream and sugar on potato chips? I asked the waiter for an explanation. To my embarrassment, he explained that this is what they call 'cornflakes', a breakfast cereal. Well, live and learn! It was easy to follow the example, and ever since, I enjoy breakfast cereal.

On board with us was the Canadian Olympic basketball team, returning from the 1948 Olympics held in England. To our amusement, as the waiters were carrying the trays high up in the air, some of these tall fellows picked up trays of food from the waiters' extended arms, and held the trays beyond their reach. We all had fun watching the much shorter waiters trying to get the trays back, jumping high without any success. The athletes finally put the trays back on the table but we had a free show, which was hard to forget.

After a few days the ocean got rough, and many people did not show up for meals. Most of our group was sick to their stomachs. I was envied because I was not affected, and I claimed it was mind over matter. My friends warned, "Don't be so cocky, it can happen to you." I resisted for a while, but eventually got sicker than a dog; the first time I had ever been sea sick. The others thought it was funny, but I did not. I felt like the ship; we both had our ups and downs.

Finally, the storm subsided and we all felt better. We crowded up on deck as all of us wanted to see Canada and Halifax showing up on the horizon. What a magnificent feeling, as we had our eyes glued on the distance, eventually making out the city and the buildings as they came into view. Finally we had arrived! The foghorns were blowing and people were cheering as the great lady slid into Dock #21. (Since then Dock #21 has become a national monument, as countless immigrants have landed there.)

Thousands of excited people were departing down the gang way, and some lucky ones rushed into the arms of waiting relatives. As we were disembarking the ship, we saw cases of wooden crates with bottles labeled Coca-Cola. Each one of us got an open bottle. I had never heard of Coke before. I took a gulp and spit it out. These savages are drinking cough syrup I thought. As time passed by I started to drink Coke also, I guess I became a "savage" too.

Two

Canada, My New Home

We waited until the Canadian Jewish Congress representatives showed up and took us into their guidance. We were greeted with a small reception welcoming us to our new home, Canada. We were overwhelmed. After my experience of being deported from my own country in 1944 and people being massacred by the Nazi Bullies, and then tossed around as unwanted refuges, it was heart-warming to be welcomed as human beings. Many times I had wondered how come nobody stood up for us during the Holocaust. Where were the righteous people? There must have been God-fearing millions, who had looked the other way and good people who had done nothing. Eleven million of us were slaughtered, denying families and people to reach their potentials as future scientists, doctors, professionals, artists, or everyday human beings. Looking the other way can create disasters as we experienced. But this time it was different, as the Canadians opened their hearts and welcomed us as individual beings.

I will never give up on humanity. My promise to Andris became my mission; publish the diary to open up the minds and hearts of thousands of people. Put hatred on the back burner, and make people realize that family should be the most important for all of us. To achieve this, we have to have freedom! But freedom is not free. Now that I have been given the opportunity to become a free man, I felt eager to become one of them, a good Canadian! The Agency had given me a new window on life. I will spread the word of family values, freedom, and that bullies must be stopped, before they become a danger to society. These were big thoughts and I did not know how I could achieve such a giant task?! Chills ran down my spine, and I knew I was on the right track. For a second I remembered Andris, who is not with us anymore. But my promise to him is very much alive. We all have to make sure tragedies like the Holocaust will **Never Again** happen. Recharged by my reinforced will, I was ready for a new life in my adopted country, Canada.

Even though we "orphans" did not have too much time to see the sights in Halifax, we were anxious to board the train going west, taking all of us to our destinations. For most of us, it was Toronto, but for Zsuzsi, it was Winnipeg, where a family was supposed to adopt her.

After we were all aboard the train, sleeping compartments were assigned, upper or lower bunk. It did not matter to me, I was happy just to be alive. During the day we relaxed very comfortably on the upholstered seats, admiring the scenery as it rushed by our windows, the magnificent Canadian landscape. I saw

Zsuzsi a fellow orphan, taken in 1948 on the Aquitania.

villages, towns, farmhouses, and farmers with tractors and horses working their fields. Cattle were grazing on the endless green farmland, and I could almost smell the hay stacks. The sweet hay smell reminded me of how Andris and I used to roll in it, on summer vacations. Yes, I had left memories behind, good and bad. Life has now rewarded me with an opportunity for the future. Life is beautiful I thought.

We exchanged stories, dreams, and thoughts with one another, occasionally switching seats. Laughter was audible as we became friends with one another. Some Canadian passengers mixed in our conversations, and we were eager to make friends with them too. It didn't take long before some of them became quite friendly, and invited us to dine with them.

I noticed Jancsi was trying very hard to befriend Zsuzsi, our youngest member. He loved to stretch stories to his favor. Zsuzsi was soaking up the conversation. She was giggling, and her blue eyes looked striking, framed by her golden blond hair. Heidy and Imre (the married couple) made a good impression on all of us, as they acted more maturely, Heidy sitting next to the window, resting her head on Imre's shoulder. Even a blind person could see that they were in love. The sisters made an interesting duo. Kitty was older, dominating her slightly younger sister, Boci. Kitty fit into the role of a mother hen. (She was the only one who had met Vera briefly in Budapest.) During the days that followed, we got to know each other even better, exchanging personal stories of our young lives.

I thought I was like a spider weaving through a web of thoughts. First of all, I knew I was on my own, and I would have to fit into a new society. We heard rumors that after our arrival in Toronto, the Canadian Jewish Congress would assist us, for a short while, and then we would have to blend ourselves into everyday life. This situation would be quite a challenge, but I loved to tackle challenges, so the thought excited me. I was not afraid of maturity, as I was well on my way to becoming an adult. I knew what I had to do, as soon as I get settled on my own, bring Vera to Canada, or even to the U.S., and of course, keep my promise to Andris, which remained my life's mission. I didn't worry about publishing my diary soon; as long as Uncle Charles was alive, I would not publish it. Of course I had the giant task to translate it into English, and it would be a few years before my English would improve to that stage.

After dinner, we socialized, getting a chance to mix with one another. It was already dark outside when the night attendants converted our couches into private sleepers. Drapes hung from the ceiling, giving us privacy. Going to bed opened up a new adventure, with all the sounds of snoring, coughing, and sneezing. Sooner or later, our tired bodies found comfort and eventually we fell asleep.

In the morning we had a long breakfast, socializing as we sat across from each other at the tables. Zsuzsi was sitting opposite, and of course Jancsi Wagner was almost glued to her. We had an interesting conversation. Zsuzsi said, "Pista, if I could have a brother, I would like him to be just like you." I must have blushed at the sudden remark.

Jancsi interrupted, "You don't need a brother, you have me as a friend!"

Zsuzsi got annoyed, "Jancsi, you are a nice guy but you are too pushy. I converse with you to pass time, but I like to talk to Pista alone. He is so much more mature."

Jancsi replied, "Pista and I went to the same Gymnasium in Ujpest where he learned to be mature, just like I did."

"Jancsi," I said, "since you brought up the Gymnazium, why did they dismiss you from classes and you never returned? I've wanted to ask you this question before, but I wanted to save you from embarrassment," I said.

He turned red as a beet, and could not say a word. Zsuzsi got to her feet and said, "Pista, let's sit somewhere where we can talk, uninterrupted."

From then on Jancsi and I were not on the best of speaking terms. (This happened just a day before arriving in Toronto.) Zsuzsi and I settled on a seat near the window. She had a serious expression on her face as she turned to me, and said, "Jancsi is such a bragger. I did not know how to get away from him. Well, I guess I've done it." She continued, "Pista, I and several others have never been in a Concentration Camp. My parents placed me in a home with a Christian family, and unfortunately, they were both killed."

I replied, "We all have our own stories, but the fact is we are both orphans, and are hoping the new world will give as an opportunity for a better tomorrow. We have this one chance, and we have to make the best of it. What happened a second ago is history, we cannot do anything about it, but the future has not happened yet, and we are responsible."

Zsuzsi looked at me. "Pista you are so mature." She made this remark with admiration in her eyes and voice. Then she continued, "Do you mind if I ask you some personal questions?"

I must have smiled. "Go ahead, I have no secrets."

Zsuzsi asked, "Tell me more about Vera, she is such a lucky girl!" She said it with a sigh.

"How did you meet her?"

I paged through my memories and replied, "After I was liberated and returned to Budapest, to my surprise, Aunt Manci and her husband, Bela a dentist, still lived in the same place as before the war, St Istvan Korut, 20. They offered to let me stay with them. On the floor above lived the Koranyi family whom we did not know. I kept noticing this cute, light-brown haired girl walking by on the upper corridor, to the apartment above us daily. I made it a habit just to hang around outside our kitchen door, with my arms resting on the railing, whenever I thought it was time for her to appear. After a while it became a habit and we looked for each other. First we just exchanged smiles. Then we started to acknowledge each other by waving casually."

Zsuzsi sighed, "How romantic, please keep on."

"One morning during breakfast, sitting around the kitchen table with Buki, my favorite fox terrier, who was waiting for a treat, Aunt Manci commented, "Pista, it is obvious you like that cute girl upstairs.""

"You are right Aunt Manci," I said. "But it would be nice if someone could introduce me to her!"

"Wait a second young man!" Aunt Manci exclaimed. "After what you went through you need help for an introduction!? Go upstairs and knock on their door, and introduce yourself! You are not a helpless little boy anymore! You are a seasoned veteran. I know you can do it!"

Zsuzsi said in amazement, "I can't believe it! Don't tell me that you were shy?"

I replied, "Girls are mysterious, one can never guess what's on their minds."

"You got that right," she replied sheepishly. "Just continue, as I'm very curious."

I continued, "That same evening as per usual, I waved to Vera, waited a few minutes, and then climbed the circular back stairs, and walked to their kitchen door. Just standing there for a second, I thought that even Andris was encouraging me, "*Go on little runt, it is a cinch.*" I knocked on their kitchen door and swallowed hard."

"Who is it?" I heard the voice from inside.

"I'm Pista Nasser, the boy from the apartment below you."

A gray-haired lady with a mysterious grin opened the door and said, "Vera, There is a young man to see you."

Vera stepped into the kitchen from the hallway, blushing. She walked toward me as I stood there. She gently extended her hand and shook mine.

"I'm Istvan, but everybody calls me Pista," I was holding on to her hand.

"Hi Pista, I'm Vera. If you let my hand go, we could both sit down."

The time flew by and before I left, she introduced me to her family.

Zsuzsi laughed. "That was funny." Then she commented, "It must have been love at first sight." She let out another deep sigh. "How romantic!"

I tried to change the subject. "How about you? Are you heading to Winnipeg?"

"Yes, in that direction. The family who has invited me to stay with them, lives in a smaller community, called Vegreville," she replied.

"Tell me more about it?" I asked her.

"I do not know much about them, but I had to send them my picture, and a short biography. They offered to let me live with them, and to assist me in continuing my education."

"Wow that was quite an offer!"

"Yes, it was hard to refuse," she replied. "That was the only reason I decided not to go to Toronto. It would have been lots of fun, to be with all of you. Pista, when you get settled, would you mind writing to me and giving me your address? You can be my big brother, if I need some advice." She opened her purse, and got out a pencil and paper, and jotted down her address. "Here is my future address, promise not to lose it."

Three

The following morning as the train pulled into the Toronto station, we were all ready to disembark. Zsuzsi was the only one in our group left behind. As we left the train, she was visible from an open window, and waved good-bye to all of us. I thought of Vera, and I wished she could have been with us.

The representative of the Canadian Jewish Congress picked us up in a mini-bus and took us to Markham St. and Harbor Ave. We stopped in front of an old, but impressive, three-storied brick building. "We have arrived, everybody out," announced our guide.

As we passed through the front door and entered our temporary home, we were greeted at the desk by a middle-aged lady, smiling and welcoming us to Toronto. My assigned roommate was Leslie Benis, also from Budapest. We had met in France after I joined the group at Jouy-en-Josas. I opened the door to our twin bedroom. The accommodations were minimal: a couple of dressers, and a shared bathroom with several other people. I swung my suitcase up on the bed and opened it. I removed a few wrinkled pieces of clothing to wear for that evening's dinner. After a quick shower, I lay down on my bed beside my open suitcase and just passed out.

"Hey, Pista! Aren't you coming for dinner?" I suddenly awoke as Leslie shook me from my deep sleep.

In the dining room there were several tables. We joined many new faces, boys and girls around our age. They had arrived days, or weeks ago, and were settled in this shelter. Leslie and I sat beside each other and excitedly discussed our current situation and what the future would hold. After dinner we were officially introduced to the others by one of our host, who informed us about upcoming activities, and meeting our assigned social workers.

After the official announcements, we mixed with our newfound friends: shaking hands, and listening to so many stories, all at the same time. I met Marko, Andris, and a few other Hungarians who were mostly survivors from the camps, like me. It was an evening full of activities, but most of us could not wait to break away. We all needed another good night's sleep to function properly again.

In the morning, I picked up my instructions at the desk. I had to meet Ms. Zolansky, my social worker, in a couple of days. I had a few Canadian dollars in the envelope which my wallet too easily consumed. Giving us money was a nice gesture and made us feel like real people. I was confident that eventually I would earn my own way, and provide for myself. The Moses' sisters joined Leslie and me as we strolled around the neighborhood. We ventured down to College Street. It was the gathering place for Jewish people, mainly new-comers, who were wide-eyed and looking around, occasionally stopping at the display windows of the well-stocked stores. Window shopping did not cost us any money. It was amazing, the multitude of imported goods representing many countries.

It was a nice sunny day so we stopped by an ice cream parlor; this luxury we could all afford. Like little kids we rushed in, and bought, for a nickel, our first Canadian ice cream.

Kitty scolded Boci, her younger sister, as she tried to lick around the top of the two-scooped sugar cone, to stop it from dripping. "Look at yourself! Mother taught you better than that!

Slopping ice cream and dripping on your clothes."

I went to Boci's rescue. "Kitty, take it easy on your little sister, let her enjoy herself. Water will remove that stain." Boci rewarded me with a grin, as we continued our walk. We stopped in front of a big grocery store called Loblaw's. My curiosity took me to the meat counter. I could not believe my eyes, and called out to Leslie, "Would you believe, they have my favorite salami? Hertz!" (It is a well-known Hungarian product.)

Suddenly we heard Kitty's excited voice, "Hey, you guys, I found Hungarian paprika from Szeged!" We rushed over, and it made us feel good, to find some connections to our old country. We kept on exploring along the street, and passed a movie theater, delicatessens, and coffee shops. It was time to head back to Markham Street, so Leslie and I turned around, while some of the others kept on going.

"See you guys later," I called out, as I just about finished the last of the ice cream cone.

"That really hit the spot." I wiped my mouth with the back of my hand. I looked up to the sky and sheepishly thought, *Sorry Mom,* in case she was watching me.

In a couple of days I took the Harbor streetcar, and headed towards Spadina Ave., where eventually I found the Canadian Jewish Congress Offices. I asked the girl at the information desk and she directed me to Ms. Zolansky's office. As I entered the office, Ms. Zolansky was sitting behind the desk. I guessed she was around thirty-eight years of age, with a trim figure, wearing horn-rimmed glasses. Her hair came to just below her chin. She greeted me with a pleasant smile and Polish-accented English, "Welcome to Canada, young man."

She reached over her desk and we shook hands. In front of her, a manila envelope lay on the desk. "Have a seat," she said as I made myself comfortable. I felt a little apprehensive about the unknown, but to me it was just another great opportunity. She opened the folder, browsing through it, and then looked at me saying, "Nasser, Istvan, Pista- quite a name. Do you mind if I call you Stephen? That is the proper English translation of Istvan."

"That is fine with me," I replied. "I have been called many names, good or bad in my life."

She chuckled, "You have quite a sense of humor! I like that." She paused for a moment, and then said, "I could call in an interpreter, if we have difficulty with the language?"

I shook my head, "If you don't mind, I'd rather practice my limited English, I have a lot to learn."

"As you wish," she replied.

The ice was broken and I felt somewhat relaxed.

She spoke very slowly, which made it much easier for me to understand her English. "We are going to keep you at the Markham facility, until we can locate a family who has a comparable background, and is willing to give you food and board, and treat you like a family member. Of course we are going to pay for you, approximately $15.00 per week. In the meantime, we are going to provide you with a small amount of spending money. It won't be much, but enough, if you budget it correctly. In a few days, we will arrange for you to have a complete physical, and a dental exam. Of course you will have no expenses to worry about; we will take care of everything." She cleared her throat and continued, "I hope you understood my English." She asked me, "Do you have any questions at this time?"

I replied, "So far I've understood every word! You are so nice and considerate to speak slowly."

Ms. Zolansky smiled, "That is my job."

I shifted positions in my chair and said, "I do have one question to ask. How soon before I can get a job? I would like to be self-sufficient as soon as possible."

Startled, she replied, "Wait a second, young man! What's your hurry? You have just arrived."

"That is true, and I'm not impatient, I would just like to become self-supporting, independent. Your agency has a tremendous task ahead of you. You would have one less person to take care of. I hope I did not insult you with my statement?" I asked with concern.

She stood up and walked around her desk, standing in front of me as I was sitting. She placed both hands on my shoulders and said, "Young man, first I liked your sense of humor, and now I admire your attitude. I predict the future will reward you! You are very mature for your age. You are not even 17. If I close my eyes I could pretend that I was having a conversation with someone much older than you."

I replied, "It is not just me. I have my brother, Andris, and my Mom and Dad watching me from above. I made a lifetime promise to my brother, before he passed away in my arms. For me to keep my promise I have to be very mature." My eyes started to tear up and I had to reach for my handkerchief. I started to sob. Ms. Zolansky gave me a motherly hug, as we both broke down.

By the time I got back on the streetcar heading towards Markham Street, my emotions were calming down. I closed my eyes and imagined seeing Andris' smiling face saying, "*I'm proud of you little brat.*" When I got back, Leslie was questioning me about my interview, so I explained to him all the information that would be important to him.

That night I didn't have my usual nightmares. Instead I spent happy dream times with my family on a picnic, as a little boy, chasing butterflies, and picking flowers for my Mom. When I woke up in the morning, I noticed my pillow was damp.............

It is amazing what a good night and pleasant dreams can achieve. In the morning I was ready to take on the whole world. To top it off I wrote a letter to Vera, about my successful days in Canada and Toronto. Of course I gave her my mailing address. In a couple of weeks, I got Vera's reply.

I did have my physical check-up at Mount Sinai Hospital on University Ave. My dental appointment was in a private dental office. I have never really liked dentists. Back home after the war, I lived with Aunt Manci and her dentist husband, Bela. I had mixed memories in my thoughts. Uncle Bela was a well-respected dentist in the city, and he taught me a lot about reading x-rays, as he used to try his newly acquired x-ray unit on me. He also predicted that the bone structure of my teeth was in good shape, and most likely, I would have them for the rest of my life. Sitting in the dentist chair here in Toronto, the technician took pictures of my whole mouth.

After awhile the dentist came in, looking at the film, and spoke to me, "We need to fill six cavities. It is no problem as your Jewish agency is taking care of the cost."

I replied, "Can I see those x-rays?"

He was dumbfounded. I knew what must have been going through his mind.

He replied, "Of course you can see them."

As he let me look at the images, it didn't take me long until I pointed to one tooth, and said. "I'd like you to fill this one only." He mumbled something under his breath. He filled the tooth, and I saved the Agency many dollars to stop him from fixing some of my good teeth, as there was nothing wrong with them.

One morning as I was passing the front desk on the way to breakfast, the attendant handed me a note saying that Ms. Zolansky wanted to see me again. I was curious to find out what was on her mind. As I entered her office, we greeted each other with a handshake.

"Sit down, Stephen. I have some good news for you. We found a family for you. They are going to visit you at Markham Street, and if it is mutually agreeable, you will move in this Sunday."

"Thank you that is great news!" I said with excitement.

Then she continued, "We are getting very close to finding a job for you, fulfilling your earlier request, to become self-sufficient." I jumped to my feet and shook her hand. I imagine my eyes and behavior expressed much more gratitude than my words.

Four

My New Home

With my suitcase, I went to Manning Street, where Mr. & Mrs. Buchanan lived.

They were the couple who were nice enough to invite me to their home. I rang the doorbell.

They must have been expecting me as I stepped across the threshold. Mrs. Buchanan received me with open arms, as her husband stood watching.

"Come in young man, welcome to our home," she said in heavily accented English. "Put your suitcase in your room, make yourself comfortable, and then come into the kitchen, and we will have a nice cup of Russian tea."

Mrs. Buchanan took me around the house. In the living room she showed me the light switch and said, "You see, if you flip it up, the light goes on, flip it down, the light goes out."

She said it with such innocent honesty, that I did not want to embarrass her by telling her that back in Budapest we were not living in the middle ages. I just thanked her for her kindness.

The house was fully furnished, not to my taste, but it was respectable. My room overlooked Manning Street. I had a comfortable dark-wooden headboard bed, a bureau, a small table with a lace tablecloth, a couple of chairs, and a mirror hanging on the wall. A door opened into a small closet. I had everything I needed. The most important thing to me was the warm welcome, and being with a family. I really missed mine. *"Well Andris, we are getting settled."*

In a couple of days, I looked up the address Ms. Zolansky had given me, for my future work. It was in a commercial area, at a small blacksmith shop. As I entered, my boss-to-be welcomed me. "You must be Stephen; I was notified by the Jewish Agency that you might be working for me." He extended his hand and said, "I'm Mr. Jim Klein, just call me Jim."

I shook his hand and said, "Thank you for giving me the opportunity to learn the blacksmith business."

Then he started to explain what my job would be. "I'm custom making iron window bars, a kind of protection against intruders. Your job will be to measure the customer's window, and here in the shop, fill the order. After the bars are completed you will also have to install them. It is quite a procedure."

I was standing there scratching my head, wondering what I had gotten myself into.

Jim must have noticed my hesitation, as he said, "Of course I will teach you, step by step. It will take training and a good attitude for you to succeed."

I thought that if he was willing to teach me, I'd have no problem with attitude; it is just a challenge, to be able to earn enough money to be self-sufficient. It is my first step in the right direction, so I said, "It sounds like a challenge, and I love challenges."

He firmly shook my hand, and with my strong grip, I returned the favor. "I like your attitude! You will start tomorrow morning. I will pay you weekly starting at $0.75 an hour," he said.

"What time shall I be here?" I asked.

"At 8:00 A.M.," he replied, "and you finish at 5:00 P.M."

The same day I wrote to Vera about my adventures, and of course, so she would have my new mailing address.

After days of thorough training, I felt confident enough to create the iron bars, and went on a few appointments to measure the jobs with my boss, Jim. He told me he was pleased with my progress.

One day, Jim was installing a downstairs bar on the living room window. I was upstairs in a bathroom, standing on a ladder, reaching high to a sky window way above the bath tub. The window bar I'd made was lying on the floor. I had to pre-drill holes into the wooden window frame. I had a heavy industrial drill in my extended hands, and was putting pressure on the long drill bit to go through the wooden frame. The ladder slipped and I lost my footing, falling all the way into the empty bath tub, breaking an ordinary drinking glass on a shelf, as I hit it with my extended arm. The crash must have been heard in other parts of the house.

This middle-aged woman rushed into the bathroom, as I lay helpless and hurt in the bathtub. She yelled, "Look what you have done, you broke my glass!"

By this time, Jim ran up and entered the bath room. He saw the situation, and exclaimed,

"What's wrong with you woman? Can't you see he is hurt, and you worry about a lousy drinking glass?"

Jim helped me out of the tub, and noticed that besides my multiple bruises, my wrist had been hurt. He helped me into his station wagon and rushed me to the Emergency Room of Mount Sinai Hospital. They found no major or internal injuries, but I had a fractured wrist and several bruises. It took a few weeks for me to recover, and, of course, that ended my career as a blacksmith.

Ms. Zolansky arranged for the medical expense coverage of my wrist injury. After my recovery she found another work opportunity for me, with a jewelry shop manufacturing gold rings. It was called Goldcraft Jeweler. The owner, Joseph Fleischman, was from Hungary.

This new job was much more to my liking, better than being a blacksmith, but like the saying goes, "Beggars can't be choosers!"

I started to earn more money, $0.86 per hour. I guess it was progress. I had no difficulty learning the trade and after several months, I asked my boss, "Mr. Fleiscman, I would like to become a diamond setter, do you think that is possible?"

He looked at me, and after thinking a few seconds, he replied, "Diamond setting is a well-paid craft. No one I know is willing to teach this highly skilled profession, unless you were born into a family where they teach the trade, from father to son. Knowing you, it would not surprise me if you could learn by yourself if given the opportunity."

I must have looked puzzled.

Mr. Fleiscman continued, "I do have to pay a heavy price, when I send out some of my rings to be set with diamonds. I can't keep an expert diamond setter here in the shop, as they get paid by the piece, and we haven't enough work to keep them busy. I have an idea. See if it sounds like something you are capable of doing. You are very good with your hands and using engravers. I can give you some old diamond rings, and you can study them and take them apart. I'm confident you can learn on your own, and of course I do have some basic knowledge, that I can share with you. If you can do that, I will benefit by having my own diamond setter here, and you could be on your way, to learning a "secret" profession."

I exclaimed," Mr. Fleischman! This is a big challenge! You are looking at your future diamond setter, thanks to you!"

He winked at me, as he replied. "We shall see, I believe you can do it."

That started my diamond setting career, and a precious stone setter. Mr. Fleiscman remained a good friend for years to come, and he even invited me for festive dinners at Jewish Holidays.

In the meantime, months became years, as time passed by.

Adusting to Freedom

Letters kept on coming from Vera. She had some bad news about Hungary; the government had turned totally Communistic and the Iron Curtain was shut tightly. At times I felt guilty, as such a beautiful young lady at her 18-19 years of age, was putting her life on hold. I'm sure she was refusing other young men, just waiting for me. First the Nazis, destroying my family, and trying to kill all the Jews. Now the Communists, blocking our future, and putting an obstacle in the way of our dreams. I must not get discouraged though; I've a promise to keep to my brother, Andris, and to Vera.

After I left Mr. Fleischman, and advanced as a precious stone and diamond setter, I was hired by Jules Newton and his Swan Jewelers. We got on very well. Mr. Fleischman was glad to hear from me, as we called each other, and I let him know how I was doing.

One day Swan Jewelers moved to Wellington Ave. Three of us were moving a heavy lath upstairs to the second floor. Since I was the strongest and had a well-developed neck, from Greco-Roman wrestling, I placed a leather belt around my neck attached to the lath. I was backing upstairs step by step, and the other two were holding on to the bottom of the lath, when one of them slipped and the whole weight jerked my neck. Sharp pain overwhelmed me. I was taken to the Emergency Room at Mount Sinai Hospital, once again. I had no internal injuries, but my vertebra was badly strained. Chiropractors eased my pain somewhat, but not enough to make any lasting improvement. Finally, I went to see a neurosurgeon. He recommended an operation, but I would not agree to have my vertebra surgically altered.

Before I said good-bye to my last hope, the doctor gave me advice, "It might take years for your body to heal itself, if ever. I recommend a couple of times a day, once at night, and once before you go to work, go into the shower, and gradually increasing the heat on your neck, let the hot water penetrate deeply. At once switch to cold water, it will shock you, but that is the best internal massage you can get. Repeat the procedure, three times. After, lie on the floor on your back, and relax about five minutes. Slowly turn on your side, and ease yourself up, to standing position. Good luck to you, I hope you can cope with it."

This was a difficult situation, but I learned to cope with it. It was hard to get up from bed and go to work. I was still setting stones, which required strict control of my arms and hands. Doing my work became very painful. I got permission from my employer to stretch out on the floor, whenever I needed some relief. The pain eased somewhat, but it still lasted almost thirteen years.

I met a Hungarian couple, Mr. and Mrs. Katona, at the local "Magyar Haz"

Hungarian House. They were very friendly to me, and after some conversations, I decided to leave the Russian family I was living with, and accept their invitation to move in with them. My new room was bright and well furnished. The home-cooked Hungarian food reminded me of my old country. Breakfast was to my taste, and at night time as I entered the front door, the smell of good, Hungarian food woke up my hungry taste buds. Paprikas, gulyas, and other familiar dishes, pleased me, sometimes followed by some good Hungarian wine. Life was great, except for my constantly aching neck. The hot and cold showers somewhat eased my misery.

Back in the Camp, I had had to fight daily just to stay alive for another day. This current physical impairment will not last forever. With determination and courage, it will get better. *Be patient Pista*, I thought.

Reading Vera's letters gave me great comfort. I did mention to her my unfortunate accident, but I didn't tell her about my agony at work. I thought she should know about my daily life but I didn't want her to share my suffering. One day on a medical visit to Mount Sinai Hospital, I got a shot of cortisone, which gave me quite some relief. It felt so good to be pain-free for a short while. In a couple of weeks I went back for another shot. (I do not believe in over medication, and I've never been on drugs long enough to become addicted.)

My neck improved to the point that at work I was able to carry on sometimes for an hour, without lying down to stretch my aching bones. I did not have much of a social life. When I felt lonely, I found comfort in Vera's letters. I just had to close my eyes, and we were once again laughing together.

One day Kitty invited me to her adopted family's house. They were very nice people, of Polish-Jewish background. Kitty had continued her education to become a teacher, as her adopted parents made it possible. It must be a good feeling, when strangers take you in and treat you like family. Her sister, Boci, was also fortunate enough to be 'adopted' by a Canadian couple.

Occasionally, I went back to Markham Street, and mixed with some newcomer youngsters. Some of them were homesick, and I found great pleasure in cheering them up.

One day, I ventured out to see my first movie on College Street; *Superman* was its title.

I had to concentrate to follow the dialogue, but I understood quite a bit of what was spoken.

Occasionally the audience chuckled, and I felt lost, but once I paid attention and followed my neighbors, I laughed at what they thought was funny. I had a good time, but I was wondering how much longer before I would get to the point, of having a good command of the English language.

When I got home, my Hungarian host asked me, "Did you do anything special tonight?"

"I went to a movie," I replied.

"What was the name of the movie?"

"*Supperman*," I stated proudly.

They burst out laughing. "You mean *Superman!!*"

I caught on and joined them in laughter, "How foolish of me!"

"You are speaking very good English, compared to most of the refugees," my host commented.

Yes, I was a refugee, and I was waiting patiently, to complete my five-year's residency, as I wanted to become a Canadian citizen. I strongly believed that if a country was good enough to give me shelter, the least I could do, is to become a proud citizen.

Five

Hard Work Pays its Dividends

Some of my friends, Miki, Szoke, and Leslie bought motorcycles. I was saving too, and when the big day arrived, Miki drove me to the cycle shop. I'd saved enough money to buy a BSA, 175 CC, a light green machine. It was my first possession, and I was very proud of it, since I fully paid for it, with no pesky payments to haunt me monthly. I held a steady job, and was doing well at setting colored stones, and diamonds. Life was good to me. The four of us were the envy of the Markham crowd. When I was sure of handling the bike, I took kids on a spin occasionally as the others just watched, while we were having a good time.

One day I had a three-day weekend vacation, and Kitty's family invited me at their summer home at Lake Simcoe, a nice resort in Ontario. Mr. and Mrs. Finestein thought a lot of me, so I had an open invitation to visit them. I packed my backpack, attached it to my luggage rack, and had an enjoyable ride to the lake. As I approached their house there was a slight breeze that ruffled the bluish green water. It was a pretty sight. I parked my bike, grabbed my bag and rang the doorbell.

I heard Kitty's cheerful voice, as she pulled the door open, and announced loudly, "Pista has arrived!" There was a young man beside her holding her hand, as she introduced him to me. "Wolfie, this is my good friend Pista, the one I mentioned to you earlier."

We shook hands, and Mr. and Mrs. Finestein appeared, walking in from the kitchen. Mrs.

Finestein gave me a friendly hug asking, "How is my favorite boy?" She continued, "Just be careful of that motorcycle," stating her motherly advice.

Kitty perked up with her usually smiling face, grabbed Wolfie's hand, and dragged him outside saying, "Come on every one! Let's see Pista's new motorbike!"

We had a nice lunch, put on our swimsuits, and stepped into a waiting rowboat, as Wolfie and I each took an oar, and rowed in tandem. Kitty kept up the conversation, as she was a natural talker. After a few minutes she pulled out a tube of sun screen, and in her motherly fashion, Wolfie and I had some cream spread on our shoulders. We stopped rowing and finished applying the cream, wherever we thought we needed protection against the sun. The water was too cool to swim in, but we all had a good time swapping stories, after Kitty slowed down and we were able to get a word into her one-way conversation. She also mentioned Vera since she knew of my devotion to her. By the time we got back, we were ready to wash up, and have an afternoon tea or coffee.

After dinner, we just relaxed in the living room, and continued answering questions about our life experiences. I was the only Holocaust survivor there. Kitty had been a hidden child with her sister Boci. Their parents died in the Holocaust and they became orphans. I felt overwhelmed with their curiosity about my Concentration Camp experiences. I explained about my diary I wrote on torn cement paper bags at the age of 13 under the nose of the Nazis. They learned how I was keeping it secret from my Uncle Charles. During my story there were many teary eyes. It was getting late and finally we all went to sleep, as Wolfie and I were physically, and all of us, mentally exhausted. We bid good night to one another.

This mini-vacation gave me the relaxation I needed. At my job I was a piece worker, getting paid by each stone I set, not by hourly wages. I was considered a good and fast worker and made a very decent wage considering my age and experience. My employer now was Libman & Shaw Jewelry. The shop had about eighteen employees; fourteen jewelers who were involved in casting the gold into mountings and then forming and shaping the castings into rings and settings. The finished product had to be rouged and polished into shiny rings. These craftsmen got paid by the hour. We setters, as piece workers, had to set the diamonds or semi-precious stones into the individual rings. We made the best money in the industry, but only if we had plenty of work. Since orders had slowed down, four of us just sat around, read books, or went home, hoping the following day would be better. Since I was the youngest setter, without any financial reserves, I sat around and waited to get an order to help me pay for my room and board.

After a few days of sitting around, my income dropped, and I had to make a decision. I was not under the helping hand of the Jewish Agency any more. I had some free time on my hands because of the lack of work, so I hopped on my motor bike, and drove around in residential neighborhoods, stopping by many 'Room for Rent' signs.

One day, while driving on Shaw Street, I stopped at a three story house, which looked very similar to the other houses in the neighborhood.

I rang the doorbell as I had many times before. This middle-aged lady opened the door, as I casually asked, "Do you have a room for rent?"

She questioned me, "Is it for you?"

"Yes," I replied.

She looked me over and in a friendly tone of voice, she invited, "Come on in young man, My name is Mrs. Alderman, what's yours?"

Pista, age 18, at Shaw St rooming house, Canada.

29

"I'm Stephen Nasser, but my friends call me Pista."

We shook hands, and she sported a warm smile. "Are you a Hungarian refugee?"

"How did you know?" I asked with amazement.

"Your accent and your name, Pista, was an easy give-away. Are you one of the Holocaust refugees the Canadian Jewish Congress brought out from Hungary a couple of years ago?"

"You are right again," I responded.

"Are you looking for room and board?"

I knew I would have like to have board also, but at this time I could not afford it.

"For the time being, I'm interested in a room only."

She must have been very sharp, as she stated, "I have a lovely double room upstairs. If you have a friend, you can share it, and it would save you some money. Follow me."

She led me upstairs, passing a bathroom. Right beside it, a door opened up to a spacious double room with twin beds across from each other separated by a large window overlooking Shaw Street.

My brain went into overtime; Leslie Benis had mentioned to me, the last time I met him going on a motorcycle outing, that he was planning to move. I answered Mrs. Alderman,

"I have an idea that might work. I have a Hungarian friend, a very decent guy. I can ask him, and I will get back to you. By the way, how much would it be for the two of us?"

"Would $12.00 suit you?"

I could not believe my good fortune that this closer location could solve my problem. After I got home and had dinner with my Hungarian family, I cleared my throat and said to my landlady, "I've thoroughly enjoyed my stay with you, and I hate to give up your welcome, but my situation has changed, and I have to cut down my traveling time to work. I have found a very convenient location much closer, so I've decided to move by next week."

There was an uneasy silence around the dinner table. She said, "Pista, we hate to see you go. I want you to know that whenever you stop by we will always welcome you as a good friend, isn't that right, Daddy?" He shook his head in agreement.

The following day I contacted Leslie, and we both went back to Shaw Street. Leslie and I became roommates. Several weeks passed by, and we started to get more orders at work, so I was able to save money for a rainy day. Leslie and I dined in neighborhood restaurants, and many times Miki and Blondie joined us. We all had motorcycles, and took several trips to the countryside, visiting the Muskoka region several times. That area was a natural wonder; while riding our motorcycles on the curving roads, at almost every turn a mysterious lake popped into view. We spotted beavers, deer, and occasionally bear. Life was beautiful.

In my private moments, I looked up and thought of Andris, waiting for an imaginary smile.

Moments like that always gave me some extra courage, and were a constant reminder to keep my promise that I'd given to my brother. *"I will share my diary with the public, and will spread the word of family values and appreciation of freedom."*

I had also made a promise to Vera. It now had been almost two years, since we had bid an emotional good-bye to each other at the Budapest railroad station. I had dated Vera since I was 15, and she was 16 ½ years of age. Her mother, Mrs. Koranyi, had cautioned Vera, "You are a very attractive young lady. You have refused to date several young men who were your age and attending University. We like Pista; he is a nice boy, an orphan and a Holocaust Survivor. You have to face facts. As your mother I'm cautioning you. While you're waiting for him, you are denying yourself many opportunities. Time flies by, think about it." Vera had confessed this to me as we were sitting on a park bench, holding hands on Margaret Island.

I had asked with great concern, "What did you say to her?"

She gave me a big hug, replying, "I told her I'm in love with you, and not interested in some stupid show-off university students." We had embraced each other.

Meeting a New Tenant

Leslie and I had just finished dinner at "Sunny Boy's Coffee", a short block and a half from our rooming house. We discussed our work usually. This time Leslie talked about his girlfriend, Marika, who was a refugee like us. "You know Pista, you are so lucky having Vera, and waiting patiently to bring her out, one day. Marika is part of my daily life, but honestly, I do not love her. I don't know what to do! It is hard to break away from her. Can you give me some good advice?"

The question hit a soft spot. "Leslie," I replied, "if you know you have no intention to marry her, don't play a game, but man-up. Tell her the truth. Don't waste her life by denying your honest feelings toward her. It might hurt her momentarily, but you will give her an opportunity to carry on with her life. She will have a chance to meet someone else, who could be best for her future."

We walked a few more steps in silence. Then he stopped, grabbing my shoulder, and said,

"Thank you, friend, you really helped me make up my mind."

We soon entered our rooming house. "Hey, boys, come into the kitchen," we heard Mrs. Alderman's high pitched voice calling to us. As we walked into the kitchen, we saw an elderly, white haired gentleman sitting at the table. "Meet Mr. Joseph Cash from London, England." We shook hands, and all of us sat around the table. Mrs. Alderman as a good hostess asked, "Coffee or tea, any one?"

Mr. Cash requested, "May I have a cup of cha?" Then he explained to Leslie and me, as we looked puzzled, "That's tea in England."

Mrs. Alderman joined us at the table, and we started to drink our coffee as Mr. Cash sipped his tea. She turned towards Mr. Cash, explaining to us, "He left his wife and two daughters back in London. They will follow him soon, and will stay with us on the third floor."

Mr. Cash curiously asked the two of us, "I was told you two lads are Hungarian Holocaust Survivors? Since we are going to live together, do you mind telling me about yourselves? I've never met anyone before who survived the Holocaust."

The conversation carried on, back and forth, until Mrs. Alderman reminded us that Mr.

Cash had had a very long day. We bid good night to one another.

A couple of days later, Leslie and I asked Mr. Cash if he would like to join us for dinner.

We met at "Sunny Boy's Coffee", seated ourselves in a vinyl-upholstered booth, and ordered our meal. I asked Mr. Cash. "Were you able to find a job?"

"I was lucky; I'm starting to work next week. My wife and I are experienced Fur Operators."

"Mr. Cash, how old are your daughters?" asked Leslie.

"Gloria is the oldest, she is going on twenty, and Elsa is 17." He reached for his billfold and continued, "I have a few photos if you'd like to see them."

Leslie eagerly reached for the photographs, commenting, "Gloria is beautiful! Is that an older photo of the younger one? She is attractive also."

He handed me the pictures. He was right; Gloria was very good looking, and Elsa's picture must have been a couple of years old. Their mother looked attractive too. I handed back the pictures saying, "Mr. Cash you have a family to be proud of."

His eyes were sparkling, as he proudly said, "They are the apples of my eye, aren't they lovely?" We thanked him for his offer to pay for our dinner, but refused, as we had learned to be independent.

Back at Libman & Shaw, business had picked up and I got more work again. My back injury didn't give me any more problems. I was able to work, with caution, and rest my back once in awhile. I even resumed my Greco Roman wrestling at the local Y.M.C.A. I did not go into competition, as I was just exercising to the point that my injury allowed me.

One night I had trouble falling asleep, after reading Vera's latest letter. "Dear Pista," she had written. "It is apparent that the Communists are not just tightening the Iron Curtain, but they're also making it more difficult to receive all of your letters, or possibly for you to get mine. It has been two long years since your departure. I'm still working as a private secretary, but my personal life has not been easy. Mother does not stop nagging me. She knows that we have made a commitment to one another. I'm sure it is not easy for you to start a new life. We just have to stay strong. Love, Vera."

I knew Vera's life was not easy, an attractive girl refusing to date, with a constantly nagging mother. As I lay sleeplessly awake, clouds of thoughts entered my troubled mind.

What if Mrs. Koranyi was right? Vera was not getting younger. She must be missing many opportunities, while she is waiting for me, a refugee boy, on the other side of the world pursuing a dream, hoping it will come true. Am I holding her back? Am I responsible if the political situation does not change? I knew I could not control the facts, but I knew I could set her free, by releasing her from our commitment to each other. The thought stabbed me in the heart. What would it do to me? And what would it do to her? There was no easy answer; either I listened to my heart, or to my inner conscience. Writing her that letter, I will lose her, but if I don't, I will be responsible for blocking her chances of finding happiness in her future. Just a few days ago I gave Leslie advice about his relationship with his girlfriend Marika, but there is nobody on earth who can help me. The decision is my responsibility. The following day, I sat down and started to write. I tore up several compositions. Finally I mailed my letter, with a heavy heart. There was no turning back. Several weeks passed by.

One evening as Leslie and I walked in from our dinner hang-out, Mrs. Alderman greeted me with a big smile, "A letter from Budapest!"

I grabbed the letter, and taking two steps at a time, I ran up the stairs, and rushed to the bathroom for total privacy. My heart was in my throat. I noticed the sender was Mrs. Koranyi.

I tore the letter open and read, "Dear Pista. I know you must be broken-hearted, so is Vera.

When she read your letter, she burst out crying, immediately blaming me for your decision.

34

Thank you from the bottom of my heart, for making such a mature decision. Vera eventually will get over this broken dream. I will see to it. But I have to commend you. You are more of a man, then she will ever find. God bless you, the Koranyi family." I was crying, out of control, as Leslie pounded on the bathroom door.

Next morning back at the shop, I concentrated on my work which gave me some relief.

I didn't want anybody's sympathy. I knew I was right, but my decision left a scar on my heart. God knows how many times after work I've returned to my room, finding comfort in pulling out my cardboard box full of Vera's letters, and just reading one after the other.

Finally, Leslie helped me to find my way back to reality. "Pista! Stop that sulking! You helped me when I needed help, you gave me a wake-up call and you were right. Now it is my turn. You made a very noble decision and you were right again. I'm very proud of you, and so is the Koranyi family. It is done and finished, now get on with your life, Buddy." He gave me a brotherly hug. All of a sudden I felt as if Andris was hugging me, saying, *"I'm proud of you little brat."*

We had a long week-end coming up. I got a telephone call from Kitty, who extended the Feingolds' invitation to me to visit at their Lake Simcoe vacation cottage. It would be a good way for me to relax and organize my thoughts. Kitty and I had a chance to talk privately.

She was the only one who had ever met Vera, very briefly, but she knew her. I told her what had happened. She was crying like a baby on my shoulder. "Pista! That was an unselfish decision on your part. I'm so proud of you."

I replied, "Thank you Kitty, but please say nothing to anyone. You and Leslie are the only two friends who know my personal life."

She said, "I'm so glad we are good friends."

I agreed. "Good friends we are and we are going to keep it that way." I made sure she got the message. Kitty and I kept our friendship, but nothing more.

Six

ARRRIVAL OF THE CASH FAMILY

It was a gloomy autumn day in Toronto, a regular workday, except for Mr. Cash, who was naturally excited. His family was flying into Malton Airport at mid-afternoon. He was going to pick them up in his newly purchased 1951 shiny, dark green Meteor.

As usual, Leslie and I had our dinner at "Sunny Boy's". As we walked home to 436 Shaw St., we knew to expect a few new faces there. Mr. Cash had been looking forward to this day, since he had not seen his family for several months. I unlocked the front door, and we heard Mrs. Alderman's voice, "Boys, come on down, soon as you have a chance. There are some people I'd like you to meet."

"We'll be there in a few minutes," I replied, walking upstairs to our room. Leslie was standing in front of the mirror, adjusting his hair. "Come on, you look very handsome," I remarked with slight sarcasm. I was half way down the stairs when Leslie finally came out of our room.

The staircase ended in the hallway in the front entrance. To the left there was a glass double door, opening to the spacious living room. Sitting on couches and chairs were Mr. and Mrs. Alderman, and their children, Maxin and Juno, Mr. and Mrs. Cash, Gloria and Elsa. Their daughter Elsa, did not look like she had in the photograph. She was more mature and quite attractive. Of course the introductions took a while; shaking hands, exchanging smiles and mispronouncing names. In a few minutes, things calmed down, and we all got seated. I smelled the aroma of fresh coffee, as it was perking in the kitchen. Leslie got seated between Mrs. Cash and Gloria, and I sat next to Elsa. Then we broke up into smaller groups, and Leslie rushed to sit beside Gloria and I kept Elsa company.

After some small talk I found out a little bit about Elsa's schooling and her last employment as she said in a charming English dialect, "After I finished high school, I studied dress designing, got work in a dress shop and even helped work on Queen Elizabeth's coronation gown."

Our conversation soon turned to my tragic past and how I had survived the Holocaust. She was shocked. "Oh my God!" she exclaimed. "You mean to say, you were only 13 when your whole family got killed by the Nazis?" She reached gently for my hand. I felt the warmth of her emotion as she tried to hold her tears back. "My poor boy, it is a tragedy."

I replied, "That happened many years ago. I promised my brother who died in my arms, that I would keep a smile on my face as long as I live, to keep my family happy watching me from above."

She got up quickly, overwhelmed by emotion, and disappeared to the washroom. The conversation came to a sudden stop, as the others wondered what had happened to Elsa. She came back in a few minutes. She had dried her tears, and washed her face, and she tried to act natural. Her mother got to her feet with a worried look, as Elsa reassured her, "I'm fine, but I'd like to ask Pista a lot of questions." Elsa smiled at me, and everybody resumed their conversations.

Mrs. Alderman called us into the kitchen. "Okay, every one, let's have some cake, coffee, and tea."

Mr. Cash added, "She makes a lovely cup of cha."

It was getting late, and before all of us retired, we had our tea and coffee with some homemade cake. Mrs. Alderman got all of our attention, saying, "Saturday evening we would like to have all of you for dinner, in honor of the Cash family."

Saturday morning Leslie and I had a small breakfast at our favorite restaurant. We knew Mrs. Alderman was a good cook and a great hostess. That evening, she made a delicious dinner of Beef Wellington and Yorkshire pudding. Occasions like this made me remember the loss of my own family. A long time ago mother, dad, Andris, and I used to have family dinners accompanied by conversation and occasional laughter. *Nowadays most people take this for granted*, I thought.

On Sunday afternoon I took Elsa to a movie. After the show we walked on College Street and sat down in an ice cream parlor. We discussed the movie, and she asked me, "Do you have a girlfriend?"

I answered without hesitation, "I do have several friends, and some of them are girls. However, I have someone special in Budapest, and her name is Vera. I've known her since I was 15 years old."

She looked in my eyes, and asked, "It must be difficult for both of you to keep a long distance relationship?"

"You are so right," I replied.

"By the sound of your voice, you are missing her a lot," she stated.

"That is putting it mildly; we are very much in love with one another." I thought, *be honest*, so I was.

She let out a sigh, and then she asked, "Are you planning to bring her out, to Canada?"

I answered her honestly, "Yes, I was, up until a few weeks ago. But my conscience has been haunting me for over a year, ever since the Iron Curtain has made it nearly impossible for her to join me. I've felt guilty and selfish, to keep her like a beautiful flower preserved, and with time, wilting away." I explained the letter I had written to Vera, and that I had gotten Vera's mother's reply.

Elsa was tongue-tied for a moment, and then she replied, "You tossed away your beautiful flower?"

"No, I didn't. I gave her a chance to bloom again. It tore my heart apart, but I thought it was the right thing to do!"

She looked at me and whispered, "You are a very kind man." We continued our walk back to Shaw Street. Before we entered the house

Elsa stopped and said, "I fully understand your feelings. Could I be your friend? I will understand either way."

I took her hand and said, "It would be nice to have you as a friend, but please understand that Vera has a special place in my heart." She gave me a friendly hug, and I had a new friend who understood my deepest feelings.

I had my work routine, five days a week, but on the weekends, Leslie, Mike, George, Blondie, and I rode our motorcycles. I'd traded my BSA, for a spanking new, bright red Jawa 250 CC motorbike. We enjoyed putting on our goggles, the fresh air cutting in our faces, as our 250 CC Jawa machines reacted to our commands, as we sped away. Mike and Blondie had minor spills, only their pride got hurt. I was a little bit more conservative, and managed to stay away from accidents. I'd asked Elsa to sit on the back of my motorbike, and accompany me on one of our outings. She would have been a good sport, but her mother strictly forbade her to sit on a motorcycle. We still went on walks and to occasional movies. She became a good friend, but never tried to become a girlfriend. We fully understood each other.

One Friday evening we decided to go dancing. Eight of us, four couples, rented a van, and drove to a local dance club. We had a great time, listening to a Big Band orchestra, and we stayed until close to midnight, enjoying each other's company. That night we all decided to plan some more trips in the near future.

A holiday weekend was approaching, and our group of couples planned a trip for two night's stay, to Lake McKellar, in the lovely Muskoka region. We had to rent a cottage to sleep eight of us, and we needed a van to drive up North. This would be our first overnight trip that we had ever organized. Heidy and Imre were the only married couple. The others had no restrictions; they were adults and had no one to tell them what to do. Of course Elsa and I were in a different situation, we would have separate beds. We had no romantic attachments, we were just good friends, enjoying each other's company. I asked Mrs. Cash and she gave the O.K. for Elsa to come with me. She had no worries; she understood that Elsa and I were just good friends.

The big day arrived. We anxiously picked up our van from Hertz. We drove past Huntsville, about 15 miles out, when Andris, who was driving, smelled smoke seeping into the van. He stopped the vehicle, and pulled off the road. We spread around the vehicle, and I noticed the rear tire on the right was smoking. It must have overheated. I checked and we had no spare tire. Some of our group looked helpless, and as I'm very quick to make decisions, I took command.

"You four girls go to the opposite side of the van. You guys come over here, we have to cool down that hot tire before it catches on fire."

Martha was panicking. "We have no water," she screamed out worriedly.

I kind of chuckled. "We don't need water, we boys have a built in fire hose! But no peeking."

Two of us at a time urinated on the tire, and it stopped smoking. Imre took over the wheel and slowly, but safely, drove back to the closest Hertz Rent a Car in Huntsville. We chose Imre to be our spokesperson. He gave them hell about the van not having a spare tire. They let us have a new vehicle, and for our trouble, we got a special discount. We had no more problems for the rest of trip.

We made several funny remarks about how we had prevented the tire from catching on fire. We sang several Hungarian songs, and for Elsa's sake we sang "Roll out The Barrel". She was the lone English girl, as the rest of us were all Hungarian. We were all tired, and dragged our luggage into our rooms. We had no trouble agreeing about sleeping arrangements. Some of us had a bite to eat. I know I had no problem falling asleep, despite the fact that the walls were not sound proof. The following day we had lots of fun preparing breakfast. We brought our own food supply. I enjoy cooking, and prepared bacon and eggs, toast, and coffee.

Heidy sounded off, "I have a good idea; the cottage is surrounded by brush. How about we all take some buckets with, and pick some fresh raspberries, and share the berries back here?"

We all liked Heidy's suggestion. As a longtime Boy Scout, remembering previous experiences, I put on a long-sleeved jacket, to eliminate the chance of being scratched by the prickly brush, and I warned every one else. Elsa and I left the cottage, but we did not have to go too far. We saw the others eagerly disappear, to begin their adventure of berry picking.

I cautioned Elsa, "If you see someone in a brown fur coat, don't get chummy with him, it could be a Brown Bear, native to this area, and they love berries also."

Elsa gave me a worried look and moved quickly very close to me. There were berries all over. We picked them gently, avoiding the prickly thicket as much as we could. One in the mouth and two in the bucket. It did not take too long, as we were getting full of berries. We stopped munching the juicy sweet fruit, and concentrated on collecting. I saw Judy, for a second, across, in-between the parting branches. The thicket was moving as she was picking the berries.

I whispered into Elsa's ear, "Don't get scared!" And at the top of my lungs, I let out my best growl, "GRRRRRRRR." Across the brush we heard Judy's scream, as she must have run back to the cottage. Elsa and I stifled our laughter.

Elsa tried to whisper to me, through her chuckles. "You are a brat!"

I nodded. "Even my brother Andris, called me, "My little Brat"."

"No wonder," she replied and pinched me on my arm.

Our buckets were getting heavy, so we headed back to the cottage. Judy and Andris were already there. We emptied our buckets into a huge container to be filled with water to wash all the berries. Judy was still shaking as she told all of us about her scary encounter with a large brown bear.

Heidy questioned her, "Did you actually see the bear?"

Judy replied, "I was too terrified, I just ran back to the cottage, as that roar was so scary."

Andris continued the story, "I heard some kind of growling that I could not make out. When I saw Judy dropping her bucket, and running for her life, I picked up my bucket and followed her."

Elsa and I winked at each other.

Then Martha questioned Andris. "Andris, you came back with your bucket empty?"

He replied, "I figured I might as well eat all the berries fresh, as there would be plenty left from everyone else."

We all took pitchers of water to fill up the large container of berries. We could not believe our eyes! There were a lot of white maggots floating on the surface of the water. We all looked at Andris as Martha exclaimed, "Hope you enjoy your share of the maggots! If you like you can have our share also." Andris turned pale, started to heave, and ran to the bathroom. We all had a good laugh. Elsa and I kept our secret about scaring Judy.

In the afternoon, some of us went fishing, and I taught Elsa the basic skills of fishing.

I caught flies and placed them in an empty match box. Back home many years ago, I had amazed people with the swiftness that I could catch a fly. We also dug for worms. We found a good spot for fishing and we caught enough fish for dinner. The girls scaled and cleaned the slimy creatures. I liked fishing, but fish was not my favorite food.

Returning from our well-spent vacation, Imre dropped us off on Shaw Street. Mrs. Cash was happy to see us returning. Elsa gave her a big hug exclaiming, "Mother, I had the best time of my life; it was just a great experience!" The following day I returned to work where I had plenty of orders waiting for me. My back did not give me too much trouble. It seemed like a new chapter was opening in my life.

Nighttime, lying in bed with my eyes closed, gave me a chance to think clearly. Tonight was a good night to re-organize my thoughts. I had eased my conscience by letting Vera live her life freely, instead of hanging onto a hopeless dream. Deeply, I knew as long as I lived, Vera would always have a special place in my heart. I also know that I am entitled to go on with my life. I lost my family and my beloved brother. I mourned them, and carried on living. I did not lose Vera; I set her free as a bird. I was the loser, by my own choice. Somehow I felt relieved that now she had a chance in life. Up till now, Elsa was a good friend, without any romantic attachment. I had a feeling, from some of her remarks that she would like to have a closer relationship, even though she respected my feelings for Vera, knowing that my love for her will never, ever disappear. Elsa was a nice girl, with loving parents and a very nice sister. To my surprise Mr. and Mrs. Cash treated me like their own son. They had expressed many times, "If we had a son, we would like him to be just like you." Finally, sleep freed me from my thoughts. I woke up truly refreshed. Even my conscience let me rest.

Seven

A Change in Life

Tonight, coming home from "Sunny Boy's", as soon as I entered the front door, I thought of Vera, my first true love. I had her box of letters and some of her pictures. One day Elsa asked me to translate one of the letters. I read some of it, but thought it was not appropriate for Vera, or me, to share our private romance.

In a couple of weeks I got some bad news. Leslie had had an accident riding his motorbike. Elsa and I visited him. He had no broken bones, just bruises, and they let him go home in a few days.

The Cashes bought a nice, two story home, on North Cliff Bl. After a few weeks, I moved away from the Aldermans, while Leslie stayed there. I now rented a room from the Cashes.

One Sunday morning Elsa and I took a bus ride to Wasaga Beach. We went swimming and sunbathed. Just past noon, we had a nice picnic lunch and some hot coffee we brought with us. We laughed, chased, and sprinkled each other with the lukewarm lake water. Soon, it was time to end our fun-filled day, so we boarded the bus back to Toronto. We had plenty of time as we held hands and conversed. "Pista, I have to confess that in the past few months I have grown very fond of you. How do you feel about me?" Elsa asked, squeezing my hand tighter.

"To tell you the truth, I have had similar thoughts about you. We have known one another for several months. We enjoy each other's company. You know my feelings about Vera; I can't erase her from my memory. If you can respect my situation, let my new life begin with you."

She looked at me, shocked for a second, and asked in a trembling voice, "I'm confused!

Is this a proposal?"

I got closer to her. "Yes, I'm asking you to get engaged."

"Yes, Yes!" she screamed out, and we embraced one another. Neither one of us cared about the on-looking passengers.

A few of them turned our way, and one remarked, "Congratulations, you make a nice young couple."

We had barely opened the front door, when Elsa yelled out, "We have some great news!" as she charged into the living room. All three of them were sitting there, Mr. and Mrs. Cash and Elsa's sister, Gloria. Mrs. Cash stood up, and Elsa almost swept her off her feet, "Mom, Pista and I are engaged!!!"

Every one was standing and I received hugs and good wishes. The excitement turned into a celebration. Mr. Cash got a bottle of liquor and glasses out of a dark mahogany cabinet.

We all raised our glasses, as Mr. Cash proposed a toast. "To Elsa and Pista, may their life be a happy and long one as a married couple."

That night, with all the excitement, it was difficult for me to sleep. With my eyes closed I imagined Andris saying, *"I'm proud of you little brat."*

The following day, back at work, I talked to my boss, Benny Libman. "Ben, I got engaged. I would like to choose a setting and diamond, and of course I will set it myself."

Ben gave me a big smile, and shook my hand. "Congratulations young man, I will give you a good discount as a wedding present."

I was very grateful, saying, "Thank you, it is very nice of you."

He took me in the show room to the display trays where there were hundreds of engagement rings to choose from. I picked a white gold ring with the center setting and places for three stones on either side.

I picked out a nice quality diamond I could afford. The only thing I needed was Elsa's ring size. I took the size chart home with me.

When I arrived, Elsa greeted me very affectionately. After dinner, with all of us sitting around the table, I said to Elsa, "I picked out your engagement ring, and all I need now is your finger size."

Elsa was eager and excited. "When can I have it?" she asked, as she had her arm laced with mine.

"Elsa, calm down," Mrs. Cash scolded her gently. "Give Pista a chance to breathe."

I answered, "I understand her, she is just as anxious as anybody else would be in her place." Then I continued, "I hate to ask, but would it disappoint you, if it takes a couple of weeks? It is our busy season."

She screamed, hitting my shoulder in jest, and jumped on me, almost squeezing the breath out of me. "You are the biggest tease, but I love you just the way you are!"

The following night when I got home, there were curious, eager eyes following my every movement, as we sat around the kitchen table. I kept up the suspense, as I fumbled around in my trousers' pocket, finally pulling out a blue velvet ring box from my pocket. I turned to Elsa and her parents and took the shiny, sparkling engagement ring out of the box. "Mr. and Mrs. Cash, could I have your permission, to get engaged to your daughter, Elsa?"

They jumped to their feet, as Mrs. Cash said, "We are losing a daughter, but gaining a son!" There wasn't a dry eye as I slid the ring on Elsa's finger.

The next few days were hectic and full of activity. The Cashes planned an engagement party at their home. The Aldermans and eight of my other friends were invited, as were the Bowmans, Mr. and Mrs. Cash's boss. My personal honored guests were Mr. and Mrs. Fleischman, my previous employer.

The engagement party was planned for Saturday at 6:30 P.M., a couple of weeks after we had announced our engagement. The Cashes really put themselves out. The party started with cocktails, English-type finger sandwiches, appetizers, home-baked cake, and cookies, and of course, tea and coffee. Mrs. Alderman asked the question, in her natural high-pitched voice, that everyone heard, "When are you two planning to get married?"

Everyone looked at us waiting for an answer. I tried my best. "We are still in the planning stages."

Mrs. Alderman questioned again, "Are we going to wait a year or more?"

I replied firmly. "It will definitely be this year."

She had more questions. "Elsa has her parents to give her away...." Suddenly, you could hear a pin drop.

Mr. Fleischman stepped to the center of the room and declared, "It would be our honor to step in as Pista's parents and give him away on his wedding day." Applause broke out. I was shocked and overwhelmed. I rushed over to the Fleiscmans. Mrs. Fleischman opened her arms, and gave me a big hug. With teary eyes I looked up to Heaven, and I was convinced my family was watching over me.

It was a lovely party! Several people approached the Fleischmans to shake their hands, but I wanted to speak to them privately. Mr. Fleischman noticed I was overwhelmed, emotionally. He stopped me, before I could say a word, "Son, I know you and you don't have to say anything. I'm sure your parents would have done the same thing, in a reversed situation." He put his arm around me and I felt I was not alone.

Preparation for the Big Event

Following the engagement party, we had a lot to plan and talk about. I decided to sell my motorcycle, since it was fully paid for. The money I got would come in handy for future expenses. One evening after dinner, we continued our main subject, the upcoming wedding. Mrs. Cash said, "Elsa, the dress salon you work at should give you a favorable price on your wedding dress."

Elsa reached for her handbag, and pulled out a sketch she probably drew earlier at work.

(The other day she had shared with me her portfolio of fashion sketches, and they were excellent.) Gloria snatched Elsa's drawing from her hand and said, "This dress could compliment a princess!" she exclaimed.

Elsa replied, "It is a fantasy drawing, I'm sure I cannot afford it."

"Pass it around, we all want to look at it," remarked Mrs. Cash.

Mr. Cash was ready to get in the conversation. "As long as we talking about affordability, I want to bring up the cost of the wedding. Rosa and I are going to pay for the whole affair including the cake and the photographer. Elsa will buy the wedding dress of her choice. Pista will cover the cost of the flowers. Gloria promised to take care of the invitations." We all looked at each other, digesting the generous offer of Mr. Cash. I turned, facing both of them, saying, "I'm running out of thank-yous, and words. Life has been very cruel to me.

I will have to readjust my thinking; there are people who are kind and well meaning."

Mr. Cash looked at me, "Son, you better get used to it, and by the way I would prefer it, if from now on you would call me dad, and Rosa, mom. Is that agreeable with you?"

I answered by hugging both of them. "Thank you, mom and dad."

After that emotional display, Gloria suggested, "Let's talk about the date of the wedding."

We tossed around different suggestions, until we came to an agreement and settled on the date, March 15, 1951. Gloria exclaimed, "Now I can order the invitations!" We all chuckled.

Elsa and I talked about moving into an apartment after the wedding. On the weekends we had fun searching the 'Apartments for Rent' section in the *Toronto Daily Star*. It was a little premature to look, but we had fun doing it. We also looked for furniture. We lived in a kind of "World of Make Believe".

One day after work we were sitting in the living room as Gloria cracked the front door open and asked for help, "Hey you guys, give me a hand!"

Both of us curiously went to the front door, where Gloria had several heavy boxes stacked one on top of the other on a two-wheeled shopping cart. "What on earth have you brought?" we asked simultaneously.

"Here are your wedding invitations," she proudly announced.

Of course, all of us were dying to see the finished announcements. She opened one of the boxes and Elsa let out a loud scream, hugging her sister. "They are beautiful, I never expected them to turn out so nice."

The days and weeks quickly passed, as the wedding date got closer. Mrs. Alderman sent out invitations to her female friends and acquaintances, inviting them to attend a Bridal Shower. Of course it was a night off for us guys. The Shower was a success. There were many gifts for our new home, wherever it would be.

The time had arrived for us to find an apartment. After looking with hope and having many disappointments, we found a two bedroom apartment above a jewelry store called Silverthorne Jewelers, located on St. Clair Ave. The location was near transportation, and we were very happy with our find. Our next move was to buy some furniture, but we had a restricted budget and did not want to start our marriage with bills. Our search finally paid off; we had everything we looked for, and no bills to worry about.

Dad had previously rented a hall for our upcoming wedding, and Elsa worked on her dream gown at the Dress Salon. I was not supposed to see it, but I sneaked a peek and it was beautiful. I rented a tuxedo, and I asked Leslie, and he agreed, to be my best man. Mr. and Mrs.

Elsa and Stephen getting married, with parents, Mr. and Mrs. Cash and sister Gloria.

Fleischman and all the others were ready for the big day. I also made arrangements to spend our honeymoon in the Province of Quebec, in the Laurentian Mountains. We were going to stay a week in Jasper, skiing.

The big day arrived. Mr. and Mrs. Fleischman picked me up early in their car and after Elsa got dressed; Dad drove all the ladies to the wedding hall. The Rabbi was ready and the ceremony began. There were quite a few people watching as we exchanged rings, and took our vows. Under the Chuppah I tread on the napkin-covered traditional glass, and everyone stood up, clapping their hands, wishing "Mazeltov".

As Mr. and Mrs. Stephen Nasser, we took the train towards our destination, our honeymoon. Upon returning, it was nice to find our furnished apartment waiting for us. We were lucky, as Gloria had a friend, Patricia Rosengarten, who wanted to rent a room, which would help us financially. She moved in with us, and we got on well. In just a few days, Elsa got a job as a saleslady in the jewelry store located below us. Our married life had started out on the right foot.

Raising our Children

I was still working at Libman and Shaw, and I had lots of extra work to take home, so I set up a jeweler's bench in my bedroom closet. It was a tight fit. I bought the necessary tools, and I was ready to earn extra money. I brought lots of orders home from work. I had a few days to set these colored stones, onyx, hematite and others, into the 10 carat gold rings. I was well respected in my trade and considered a fast worker. It gave me an opportunity to save some money, to buy a good used car, and later to put a down payment on our first house.

I bought a 1948 Plymouth. We were as happy as little kids, to own and pay for our first car. In 1953, we bought a brand new, single story house with three bedrooms, and a full basement. The purchase price was $12,500.00. Finally we had established our credit in Canada and we got approved for a $9,000 mortgage. Our house had no garage, but there was enough space to park on our own property. We were very happy to live in Suburbia.

The year was now 1954 and we had good news for our family. Elsa was expecting our first child. Daryl Andrew Nasser was born in Toronto on March 12, 1955, weighing 8 ½ lbs.

We adjusted rapidly to becoming responsible and loving parents. Elsa became a stay-at-home mother.

We had bought the house without landscaping. The ground was graded, but the front and back yard needed lots of work. We wanted to finish our front yard first before even starting on the back yard. It was hard work for both of us. We built a terraced rock garden with white and mauve flowers, the envy of our neighbors. The back yard was my next project. I wanted to be sure that by the time Daryl became a toddler, the yard should have grass and be fenced.

In late 1955, I traded my old Plymouth, for a spanking new 1955 Meteor. We were very proud of our new vehicle. Daryl was over a year old when I started to lay the grass in the back yard. It was a rainy day, and the rolls of grass were soaked in lots of water. It was a challenge for me to finish the job. The drizzle did not stop me from opening the large cardboard box of the swing set I had purchased on sale a couple of weeks ago.

As Elsa and I were standing in the open back door, enjoying the fruit of my hard labor, she looked at me, saying, "Look at you, you are a mess! Soaked to the skin and covered with mud! Go and have a hot shower, and dinner will soon be ready." I didn't need much urging.

Beside the kitchen, we had a small dinette. It was not furnished to my liking. We had two chairs, a table, and Daryl's high chair. I sat down all cleaned up, and began to eat after feeding Daryl. Elsa said, "Don't you feel like a new person?"

"I was a mess," I answered. While eating, I had a good idea. "I just figured out how to convert this little dinette into a comfortably built-in curved style booth, like they have in nice restaurants."

Elsa scolded me. "For God's sake! Are you ever going to relax? You do have wonderful plans, but you are only a person. Working a fulltime job, bringing work home, laying grass, and while we are having dinner, your imagination runs away. You must be exhausted! I know your answer, "I don't get tired"."

I smiled and said, "You've got that right!"

Every morning I drove to work in downtown Toronto. It took nearly three-quarters of an hour, depending on the traffic. Most of the time Elsa prepared my lunches, but occasionally I ate out with fellow workers, in some of our favorite restaurants, like the "Hungarian Csarda", or "Zuchter's Deli".

Lately I had developed a cough I could not shake, and sometimes I even coughed up some stuff, I didn't like. I did take cough medicine and over the counter drugs. I just had a chest cold, I thought. One day driving home from work, I saw a mobile, chest x-ray unit at Lawrence Plaza. I stopped by, and they also took a sputum test, beside the chest x-ray. After getting home I casually mentioned my stop to Elsa. She commented, "You must have gotten sick while you were laying the grass."

A few days later, I got a letter. "Mr. Nasser, you tested positive on your sputum. Report for further examination at the Toronto Hospital for T.B." We were both shocked, reading the letter over and over again.

Eight

We dropped Daryl off at my in-laws and drove to the hospital. After several more tests, and evaluations, we were told to wait in Dr. Garret's office. As he entered the office, I judged him to be around fifty years old, and when he spoke I detected a French Canadian accent.

"Mr. and Mrs. Nasser, I'm Doctor Garret." He picked up my chart and scanned a few pages, then he continued to speak. "May I call you Stephen?" he asked me.

"Of course," I replied, waiting anxiously for what he had to say.

"Your x-ray revealed a calcified spot on your left upper lung. It might be an old scar, and we are considering its removal. We have a Board of Doctors' meeting weekly, and they are the ones who make the recommendations, judging each case on an individual basis. Of course the final decision will be yours. It might take a couple of months before we get to that stage. Getting back to the results of your skin and sputum tests taken earlier at the mobile unit, we're positive.

All indications suggest that you have tuberculosis. Your family members are required to be inoculated with a B.C.G serum. It is mandatory under Canadian health regulations that you stay for at least 365 days in our facility. Do you have any questions?"

We were speechless. Finally I asked, "What happens if we can't afford the cost?"

"The cost of your hospital stay is fully covered by the government. If you need some personal help, you can apply for welfare, through our social facilities. They have a local office here. Stephen, you will be admitted today, and your wife can bring back some of your personal belongings."

Elsa asked, "When can I visit him, and can I bring our son with?"

"As long as your husband tests positive, it is out of the question."

We were helpless. Fate had given me another blow. I had to switch my mind into high gear to think positively. I knew I would get through this major setback, and I had to be strong enough for both of us. We still had a few minutes before Elsa had to leave to bring me back my belongings.

Elsa looked devastated. Holding on to me with desperation she asked, "What are we going to do? We have the mortgage and the car payment. Now, no income, the baby and I, and you hospitalized for a year, with T.B."

I held her tight and remarked, "This is a major problem, I've told you many times, I have no problems, only challenges. Trust me; we will get through this mess together, and one day we will look back from a much happier position. Our future is still ahead of us."

She looked at me and replied, "I know you came through hell. With you beside me, we will make it." I discovered a positive twinkle in her eyes.

Soon after Elsa left, I was assigned to my ward. As I stepped through the door, I saw five beds, with a night stand beside each. Also, there were some cabinets to store our personal belongings. My bed was the second to the right as I entered. There were three beds against the wall, and across, three more beds were standing in front of two large windows. Through the windows, I saw an old maple tree and several playful squirrels jumping from branch to branch. This was going to be my home for the next 365 days. I remembered back to 1944, when I lost my freedom and my family, and I almost lost my life. I had to be thankful that my circumstances today were beyond comparison to 1944. With the right attitude, the time would pass, and we would be one happy family again. I dared the world to try to stop me; I would recover. This was only a temporary setback. I would continue on my way, raising my family.

Elsa brought my belongings. Before we said good bye, I told her, "Listen carefully, here is my plan. I'm sure mom and dad will assist you. You have to rent the house for one year. The rent will cover the mortgage, and give you a little extra. The car has to be returned to the dealership, with as little loss as possible. I will call them from here and negotiate a good settlement. After I get out we will buy another one. You will have to move back with Daryl to your parent's house for the time being. You are very handy at sewing, and with the new machine you got, just continue sewing. You were very good at doing alterations. I don't want to go on welfare, we don't need hand-outs. We have our pride, and with the help of God, my best Friend, looking down on us, we will be on the right track."

Elsa tried to kiss me.

"Not yet, just in case I have T.B., but I'm not so sure I do."

"What do you mean?" she asked.

"Just trust me, I have a gut feeling."

"Pista, your attitude is amazing!" she exclaimed.

"Without this attitude I would not be alive today, and I also have to keep my promise to Andris. He told me, "*If you want to keep us happy up there, just have a smile on your face, and we will smile back at you.*"

She gave me a tight hug and said, "Don't worry, we will be fine." Those were her departing words.

I took my belongings back to my room, where an elderly man was changing the bedding on my bed. "Hi, my name is Cecil, you must be Stephen Nasser?" He greeted me. "I will be taking care of you, if you need anything just let me know. Your roommates are somewhere on this floor, you can introduce yourself when they come back."

I checked around my surroundings; we had a bathroom and shower adjoining our room. I got out of my clothing and changed into pajamas. I was lying in bed when I heard a new voice. This stocky lady in a white uniform entered the room, saying with a cheerful voice, "I'm Nurse McIntosh, you must be Stephen Nasser. I will call you by your first name. I'm your charge nurse. You better be nice to me! I will give you your daily shot, and medication for as long as you stay here. On your night table you will find a glass jar with a lid. That's for your daily sputum. You will meet a social worker, who will explain all the activities available for you during your stay. It is time for you to turn over and we are going to have our first shot. There, you see, we could hardly feel it."

I corrected her, "You meant YOU could hardly feel it."

She chuckled, "We have a comedian here."

Several people entered the room and sat on their beds. Mrs. McIntosh introduced me,

"Hey fellows, your new roommate is Stephen Nasser. You can introduce yourselves," she said as she left the room.

Pista at T.B. Hospital with room mates

On the bed next to me, a young Chinese boy was grinning. "I'm Harry!" He looked around 18 years old.

On the bed across from him a baldish man, around 50, said, "I'm Eugene Somogyi, but everybody calls me Smoky."

"You are Hungarian!"

"How can you tell?" he asked.

"By your name and accent."

Smoky asked, "Your name is Nasser, where are you from?"

"Budapest, Hungary, born and raised."

He looked me over and said, "That is not a Hungarian name."

"You are right; we were the only Nassers in Hungary, for at least three generations."

Sitting on the next bed, from Poland, was Joe; next was Hans from Holland, a tall Dutch boy with blond hair. He was in my age bracket. The sixth bed was empty.

Our days started with using the sputum bottle and then a shot from Mrs. McIntosh, followed by breakfast, wheeled in on a cart. Then there were visits by resident doctors, and our blood pressures and temperatures were taken by nurses' aides. Several patients kept busy with some crafts, such as leather wallets, brass plaques, bead-making, and custom jewelry.

The days that followed gave me opportunities to learn some of these crafts.

Elsa came to visit me and I told her my good news. "All my sputum tests came back negative!!!!"

She embraced me. "That's great, that means you are coming home!"

"I wish that were true. Despite the negative results, I will still have to stay for the year. It just means that I'm not infectious."

"That means I can kiss you." She didn't wait for an answer. As we embraced, she continued, "I also have some very good news. The house is rented with a year's lease, to a nice young couple. I moved in with mom and dad, and we are all settled and comfortable, and Daryl is a good baby."

It was my turn to speak. "I called the car dealer we bought our car from. After some debate, he eventually agreed to take the car back, and to release us from our contract. Originally they wanted $800.00, but finally we agreed on $200.00. Would you give them a call to return the car? Make sure you get the release."

Elsa was relieved that we were able to see some daylight, and relieved of some of our financial burdens. She was happy to inform me that the neighbors of her parents were delighted to learn that Elsa was doing alterations. As we said good-bye, she remarked, "I learned from your attitude, I feel so much better."

I had lots of free time on my hands, so I enrolled in a bookkeeping course. I also became very good at making leather wallets. I made one for Elsa, dad, and mom. I also made a lovely red clutch purse, with Elsa's raised initials on it in black leather.

I noticed most of my roommates were losing weight, related to the sickness. Myself, I felt good, gained a little weight, and never had a positive sputum. At my weekly consultation with Dr. Garret he got serious, and said, "Stephen, we had our meeting with the Doctors.

They recommended an operation, for removing a lobe of your lung, where they found that calcified spot. We had several opinions, and none of us could identify the nature of it. They felt that if it is hiding the T.B. infection, it could open, and cause you a major problem. It could be non-curable. If we remove that threat, you could be free from problems in the future.

If you agree to have the surgery, we would operate as soon as possible. That way you would have a chance for total recovery from the surgery, and still be able to leave the hospital, cured, at the end of your year. Take your time and think about it. Talk it over with your wife, and then give me your decision."

"Doctor Garret," I replied. "It has been on my mind, not just whether I needed an operation, but that no positive results have been detected from my daily sputum samples.

I believe I might have the answer about that mysterious, calcified spot."

He pulled up a chair and remarked, "I'm ready to listen."

I started, "You know that I was in a Concentration Camp. During that period I lost a lot of weight, and almost died, because of beatings, hard labor, and lack of food."

He nodded, "Terrible times in your life."

I continued. "During this period when I was so weak with hardly any resistance left in me, the Nazis assigned me to an enclosed facility. I had to shovel loose cement into large paper bags. The clouds of fine powder were thick in the air that I had to breathe. This went on for almost a week. I remember having coughing spells, and spitting out the cement. Tell me honestly, is it possible, that the cement I breathed in, settled on my lung and calcified, creating the mysterious spot?

He looked puzzled, and thought a few seconds before he answered. "Son, that is quite a theory. It puts the whole situation in a different light. It sounds like you might be on the right track. We know that with the operation, the spot will be gone. Without the operation, you will always live with a mysterious spot on your lung. Just weigh the situation, and give me your final answer. I will present it to the board. You have given me very important facts about your background."

I spent a few sleepless nights. During Elsa's frequent visits, I never mentioned to her the possibility of a serious operation. She was successfully holding the "home front", as Daryl was progressing from being a baby, to developing into a toddler. I had the pleasure of hearing about his first steps and adventures. I even saw a few snapshots; he was my pride and joy. I decided not to tell her anything about my conversation with Dr. Garett, until the final decision was made.

She had her hands full and did not need any more stress.

A few days later I had my crucial meeting with Dr. Garett. His face did not show any indication of what he had to say. "Well, young man, I had a discussion with the other doctors.

To start with, all of us were favoring an operation. After I got the background information from you, I shared it with the other doctors, and some of their opinions have changed. Have you made your decision?" he asked.

"Yes, I have," I replied. "I definitely reject the operation. I will take my chances to live with the spot."

He smiled and extended his hand to shake mine. "I'm on your side, if I were you I would have made the same decision. It's unexplained how you got that positive result on your sputum test at the mobile unit, before we admitted you. Since you have been here, all your tests have been negative. I will recommend that you get passes, to spend a little time with your family. Any questions?" he asked me with a smile.

"Yes, Doctor. Since my situation has changed, could I be discharged before my year is up?"

He shook his head, "Unfortunately, no. Health regulations require us to keep you for the full year."

I could hardly wait to tell Elsa the good news. My first visit home was a wonderful experience, to see Daryl again after half a year had gone by. I had a chance to pick him up and hug him. "Look at him, how he has grown!"

When I heard him say, "Da, da," tears of joy ran down my cheeks. My visits were short, and I could hardly wait until the next one.

I decided to build a special boat for Daryl, one that he could enjoy in later years while growing up. Back in the hospital, I started to design a model boat. Using my imagination, I wanted it to be very detailed. I drew several plans and eventually I was satisfied with the design. It was a catamaran speed boat, driven by an airplane propeller mounted on the rear stabilizer. Johnny, the Dutch boy, got interested in my project and he started to build a similar model boat. We were able to buy some balsa wood from the Hobby Supply. My design was about 28" long and the sleek body was painted red and white. After a couple of months, I finished my project.

The new year of 1957 was just around the corner. I still had about six more months to go. I read many books, exchanged stories with room-mates, and I enjoyed watching the playful squirrels, chasing each other, jumping from branch to branch. God knows how many pills I'd taken, whether I needed them or not! My sputum tests were all negative. My highlights were visiting hours, and I waited impatiently to get my passes and visit with my family, and have some time to play with my little son. I had a goal to live for and I believed I had no problems, just challenges.

I got a pass for March 12th, to celebrate Daryl's second birthday. It was a pleasure to see him with cake smeared all over his smiling face. I had a right to be bitter, because of my situation, but I had to hold it within me. I could not burden my family; they had a hard enough time making ends meet. Elsa was busy sewing. The word about her good work spread around the neighborhood, and she had lots of alterations to complete. I also kept busy, and received a few orders to make leather wallets. We all made the best of our situations.

In the meantime, Harry and Johny got discharged. They were considered cured, since they had no positive sputum results for the past three months, and their year was up. I knew my stay was the after-effect of the Concentration Camp, but those damn Nazis were not going to get me down. I was as strong as ever. I knew no General Patton could liberate me now. I just had a few more months. I challenged the world to stop me! Once I got out, I would build a new future despite of my set-back. I knew my spirit and self-confidence would not be broken.

Less than a month before my discharge, I made contact with Libman and Shaw. They would be glad to have me back at the shop, as soon as I was available. Elsa was in contact with our tenants, and our moving back to the house was arranged. The hospital was working on my release papers. I had no problem qualifying, as my tests had been negative since I entered the hospital. In my mind, I was not negative or bitter about my hospital stay.

Nine

BACK TO OUR HOME AGAIN

The day we had been waiting for finally arrived and dad picked me up. It was almost as memorable as when I had been liberated from the Concentration Camp. Yes, I had lost another year of my life, but this time my family and my own home were waiting for me.

After a few days back to normal living, I returned to work. Every morning I had to walk over a half mile to take the Bathurst bus to work. After a couple of weeks, we decided and bought another used car. This was an old Chevy. It wasn't anything like my '55 Meteor that I had been forced to return, but I knew that, with patience and determination, our future was wide open.

I set up my work bench downstairs in the basement. I had gotten some extra work to take home, and I was back in business again. For quite a while, I considered manufacturing custom jewelry as my side business. We had a large basement divided by a wall into two portions with plenty of room to set up another workshop and still have space for a recreation room I could build. To manufacture custom jewelry I needed an overhead pulley system and a long heavy work table about 10' long. I bought a one-horse power electric motor to drive the pulley system overhead. Fixed on the bench, I had a polisher grinder, a large vertical drill, and at the end of the bench, I built a tumbler, to take the custom jewelry, and tumble it to an acceptable finish. I completed this set up in a couple of weeks.

My friend "Miki "Friedman, was willing to take our sample line to jewelry stores, and we were successful at making a profit. Additionally, we partnered with another friend, Paul Ungar, and imported some designer sweaters. This adventure brought in a little more income. Financially, we were making good strides.

We bought a new car, a Rambler Wagon. Elsa fell in love with the two-tone, soft yellow accented by wooden panels. We were progressing by giant leaps. Elsa was pregnant, and we were expecting the new baby in October. In my "spare" time, I finished building Daryl a lovely bedroom with shelves and drawers, half-way around with a headboard, finished in "Roxatone", a newly introduced paint finish. I tiled the floor with vinyl, creating the feeling that you were stepping on clouds as you walked in his room. Opposite the door, above the shelves, I made the wall into a giant world map, outlining the continents with a thin white rope. In the corner I built a coat hanger shaped like a giraffe's head, protruding from the wall at hip level, finished in highly lacquered colors. His room came out better than I had hoped for.

It was time to finish the new baby's room. On October 6, 1957, we were blessed with a baby girl whom we named Michele Kim. As I was getting her birth certificate, I could not spell Kimberly in English, so she had to settle for Kim. Later on, she always teased me about my mistake. Both of our children were Canadian born. I had earned my Canadian citizenship while Elsa retained her British papers.

The Canadian winters were very cold, so in early December Elsa and I were dreaming about emigrating to the U.S. I mentioned my plan to Paul and Andy, who were also Hungarian diamond setters. They were both enthused. Three of us took advantage of the holidays, and left Toronto in Andy's car. We had only nine days, starting out a day after Christmas. We drove to Los Angeles with the three of us alternating at driving. We stopped at restaurants to eat, freshen up, and to stretch our legs. We made it there in three days, but it was a hard drive. I will always remember January 1st in Disneyland. The temperature was 81 F; what a gorgeous day! I had my mind made up. I would come to the land of opportunity, and the home of the Statue of Liberty. I thought of Andris again. *Yes, I'm keeping my promise, despite all the setbacks.* We arrived back in Canada around 2:00 A.M. at my house, and Andy dropped me off.

Emigrating to the U.S.

It was way below freezing, as I walked up our snow-covered pathway. I rang the doorbell, and in a very short time the door flew open. Elsa and I embraced each other, speaking very quietly, trying not to wake the children. I asked, "How are the children?"

Elsa answered, "Michele is well, and Daryl is having fun in the snow, but I'm cold as always."

I quickly answered, "This is our last winter here, we are moving to Los Angeles!"

She jumped to her feet excitedly, "Tell me everything!" As I went into the small details, she realized I was exhausted. "Let's go to bed, you need your rest, I can wait till the morning."

It was a unanimous decision; we would sell the house and move to Los Angeles. We broke the news to mom and dad, who had mixed emotions. They were happy for us, but sad about missing the family and grandchildren.

However, we ran into a snag with immigration. The Hungarian quota was full since the 1956 uprising in Budapest, but the good news was that we qualified under Elsa's British citizen- ship. We filed the application and sold the house. I fashioned the wagon's spacious back into two sleeping compartments padded with the appropriate sized mattresses for the children. Michele had her baby car seat and we were ready to go. I had no job, nor anywhere to stay. Some of my friends thought I was crazy, taking such a chance without securing a job and housing arrangements. They did not know me well enough. I was never afraid of the unknown, and I had enough self-confidence that I would make swift decisions, when it was necessary. We were going to make the long drive into a three-week's vacation, taking time out for many stopovers. We said our good-byes and got on our way at sunrise. We felt like two excited kids, ready for an adventure. The children were tucked into their small, but comfortable, sleeping compartments. We were heading toward our future home, somewhere in California. Stopping at the U.S. border, the border guards found our papers in order. We headed south to places we had never been, and in a couple of days we were out of the Snow Belt. I did most of the driving, but Elsa helped me out a lot. We stopped at several places for roadside pony rides, merry-go-rounds, and other attractions that entertained our young son. Michele was happy and comfortable in her stroller, watching her brother having fun. We made it a rule not to drive more than four hours a day.

We stopped by motels and occasionally drove into towns to do some sightseeing. Daryl enjoyed getting a lot of attention; we even gave him some responsibility, to feed his little sister from a bottle. During the drive, he sat on the back seat beside Michele in her car seat. He held the bottle to her as she giggled at her big brother, when he missed and the nipple slipped out of her mouth. Of course Elsa was within reach, to help. He enjoyed feeding his little sister.

Occasionally we stopped at rest areas and had picnics. Daryl enjoyed chasing birds and pigeons. Of course, it was a constant responsibility to keep him at a safe distance, but still give him some freedom, to have his fun.

We drove south until we reached Highway 66, the well-traveled road toward California. We stopped to see many sights, at petting zoos, and exhibitions of all kinds. I let Daryl help me hold the tire gauge, when I stopped occasionally. He felt so important doing it; I stopped even if we did not need to check the tires. We were lucky with the weather, though we did stop three times, and checked into motels because of heavy rain.

Highway 66 was the same route I'd driven a year before with Andy and Paul. I was the only one of the three of us who made the big decision to move to California. Of course this time our trip was a vacation taking close to three weeks. Elsa could not believe that before, we three had driven it in three days, day and night, stopping only for necessities.

The following day we continued driving. We stopped at Hoover Dam and marveled at one of the Seven Wonders of the World. We were going to stop at Las Vegas, and while I was driving, I figured out a sure way to beat the Black Jack table. Elsa questioned me, "How much are you willing to gamble to make your fortune?"

"A maximum of ten dollars," I replied.

We were excited pulling into Las Vegas and getting a room for $8.50 at the Hotel Royal Nevada, where we stayed for a couple of days. We all put on bathing suits and relaxed on lounge chairs beside the swimming pool, and I ordered a Shirley Temple for Daryl. I can still remember that grin on his face, sitting on the lounge chair, as the waiter handed him the drink. I took him swimming and then we all dressed for dinner, at a Chuck Wagon Buffet, at the Hacienda Hotel. We all enjoyed Las Vegas.

Elsa stayed in the room with the children, while I was going to outsmart the Black Jack table in our hotel's casino. As I was leaving she called after me, "Don't wake me up, if you are late getting back to the room."

First I looked over the tables playing Black Jack, and picked my dealer. I was playing the $1.00 bet. Less than ten minutes later, I walked back into our room.

Elsa asked curiously, "Did you forget something?"

My answer was short, "Yes, I left my luck behind, they cleaned me out!"

She burst out laughing. "Are you going to try to win it back?"

I answered, "You must be kidding! It was hard enough to earn our money, so we will keep it safe in our pockets, and let them find another sucker."

We left Las Vegas early in the morning. We were about 300 miles from downtown Los Angeles, our final destination. I planned to arrive in the early afternoon and find us a hotel room. Leaving Las Vegas, at Prim, Nevada, we entered California. I jubilantly blew my horn to celebrate our arrival at our final destination, California. It had taken us less than three weeks, and it was a memorable trip.

We drove through some mountains with an elevation of over 4,000 feet. We passed through Barstow, and then we saw signs for Roy Rogers' Ranch near Victorville. Finally, we arrived at the notorious Cajon Pass, which during the winter time could be a treacherous down grade. Past San Bernardino, traffic got much heavier and an hour and a half later we entered the famous Hollywood. Driving on the freeway I saw a sign advertising the Hollywood Hotel. I pulled off the freeway ramp, and drove into the hotel's parking lot. We checked in for a few days.

I decided to buy *The Los Angeles Times*, and in their "Apartments for Rent" section, Elsa and I searched for a seemingly suitable place. We studied the local maps, and in a couple of days, we found an apartment in the Glendale area. We saw three apartments available, and we choose the one we liked, that looked safe for the children. It had a playground with swings. We rented by the month. We all got settled, and in a couple of days, I started to look for a job. I called a few jewelry manufacturers, and found out that the trade in California was nothing like it was in Toronto. It was more of a family trade. No diamond setters were needed.

I did get a temporary part time job. It took me nearly an hour to drive to it, and I earned just a few dollars. I had to make a major decision. *The Los Angeles Times* 'Want Ads' solved my problem, as I decided to open a restaurant. Searching through the business opportunities, I found several interesting ads. One of them was on Colorado Boulevard in Eagle Rock, less than two miles from our apartment.

In our bank account we had a good reserve saved from the sale of our house. One location looked very favorable. The empty ice cream parlor was a fairly large corner building surrounded by a parking lot for about 18 cars. It was a former 'Frosty Freeze'. I met the previous owner who wanted $8,000 for the good will and all the used equipment in the facility. He still had a two year lease left. I met the landlord, and he was willing to give me a new five year lease, renewable for five more years. It sounded promising, but I did not want to spend all of our reserve.

I needed a partner to split the cost. Dad informed me that one of his friends, Dave Cohen, also an Englishman, had moved to Los Angeles, and was looking for a business opportunity. I met Dave, who was old enough to be my father. He had the money, the willingness, and looked honest enough. We came to an agreement, bought the place, and signed the new lease. We paid a down payment, and signed a contract to pay the rest in three years. Dave did not know anything about cooking. I didn't know much more except, as a Boy Scout I knew somewhat about campfire roasting. We got busy remodeling the place, and making sure all of the equipment was operational. I needed to gain some quick experience. I bought my favorite paper *The Los Angeles Times* and found an ad; a restaurant was looking for an experienced chef.

I drove to MacArthur Park where the owner interviewed me. "Where did you work before, and how much experience do you have? We need someone urgently."

I gulped, and said, "I came from Toronto, Canada, where I worked at the "Hungarian Csarda" and "Zuchter's Restaurant"." (I named the two restaurants where I used to have lunches.)

He replied, "I have no time to check your resume, but if you come in tomorrow morning and show our chef what you can do, I will consider hiring you."

I knew I didn't have a chance, but I had survived many obstacles, and this was another one. I answered without hesitation, "That sounds fair enough. But I would like to make a suggestion. I've trained several new chefs myself. I think it would eliminate a lot of time and misunderstanding, if I watch your chef the first day, and then I can show him I can do it the way he wants it to be done. This way you will know if I'm suitable or not, without wasting any valuable time."

He reached for my hand saying, "I like your attitude, see you tomorrow morning." We shook hands.

When I told Elsa what had happened, she could not believe I was going to actually follow through. The next morning, I showed up ten minutes early. I was armed with my determination, and a positive attitude, and I thought, *Andris is watching me from above.* That day, I watched every move of the chef, and even tried to read his mind. When he questioned me, I answered promptly. The following day it was my turn to show if I could qualify, and I got the job.

On Saturday evening the owner came to me, and said, "Young man, I'm so glad you stopped by for a job, we want you permanently."

I answered, "Sir, unfortunately something has come up, and I cannot come back, I'm very sorry."

He looked disappointed and said, "Whenever you solve your problems, I would hire you back without hesitation."

I felt guilty about deceiving him, but I had desperately needed some experience. My family and future was at stake.

Ten

OPENING MY RESTAURANT

The following Sunday, we had the successful grand opening of "The Sizzling Platter Steak House." I still did not know that much about cooking, or running a restaurant, but by getting experience from working for six days, I knew more than I had a week before. I quickly learned the skill of cooking. It took about a year before Dave had enough confidence to do the same. That was a relief, as we were able to take alternate days off. By the end of the year, our landlord agreed to build a dining room. We furnished it with upholstered booths, and bought a nice electric sign with our emblem on it, a little chef holding a sizzling platter. We boosted our seating capacity up to 60 people.

One day I had to climb on top of our flat roofed restaurant, as the old swamp cooler was not working right. We did not have a ladder to get up on the roof, but that did not stop me. I put a few tools in my pocket, and climbed on the shed door. It was a wooden structure attached to the back of the restaurant, outside the kitchen. After I got up there, my partner came looking for me.

"Hey Stephen, how on earth did you got up there?" Dave asked.

"I just pushed the door close to the wall under the roof and I climbed up. This darn cooler is on the bum, somebody has to fix it and

I know it won't be you. While you're here, bring me the hose, I need some water to fill up the cooler. He disappeared while I was fixing the connections. A few minutes later I heard a thud. He had tossed the green, coiled water hose up on the roof. He didn't have enough logic to connect the hose to the water faucet below. There was no connection on the roof.

I lay on the flat roof looking down and yelling, "Dave, Dave! Can you hear me?" My throat was getting dry from yelling.

Finally Dave came out the back door. "What's your problem?" he asked.

By now I was upset! "My problem is your stupidity!" I threw down the unconnected end of the hose. "Connect the darn hose before you disappear again. I haven't got all day to spend up here in this hot sun!" I had my hands full keeping the place in shape.

One day I told my partner, "You are not much help, but at least I can trust you." We had five waitresses, and hired a young boy, Billy, as a dishwasher, who turned out to be very reliable. He asked me several times about my former life, and I felt that he had a lot of respect for me.

After a while, I learned to butcher my own meat and cut it into different cuts. The restaurant business was very demanding, with late hours and hard work. Only Dave and I were doing the cooking, both of us during busy nights. We also had Helen, a Dutch Indonesian lady we had hired, and she was great. I really respected her, as she was able to handle charbroiling the steaks, hamburgers and grilling many other items.

We communicated with mom and dad who had made the decision to leave Canada and follow us to Los Angeles. We helped them find a very nice, gated retirement community in Seal Beach. They moved into a one bedroom condo, with many facilities offered by the community. We invited them over quite often, to be with the grandchildren, and spend some time with us and eat at "The Sizzling Platter".

Our business held its own and we were able to save a little money. We closed the restaurant every Wednesday; family day for us. We drove down to Seal Beach, had dinner with mom and dad, or took the children to

Disneyland and Knott's Berry Farm. Sometimes we just relaxed and had a family discussion. Mom mentioned, "You children should think about buying a house."

Elsa remarked, "We are looking around for a good location at a great price. We found several, brand new, lovely homes, all fenced with front yards that are landscaped, quite close to where you live."

"Then what's stopping you? It sounds just perfect," she said.

I replied, "The buying price is no problem; it is the down payment that makes it difficult."

Dad answered, "Don't worry about the down payment, how much do you need?"

I said, "It is very generous of you to offer us help, but if we wait another year, by then we could save enough, to make the down payment on our own."

He got visibly disturbed, "Rosi, do you hear this nonsense? We have the money, but he would rather wait a full year to be independent!?"

Mom spoke up turning to Elsa, "This will be a loan, and we would like you to take it. You can show us the model you like. We are not that young anymore and we'd like to share your dreams with you. We hope you can move into Rossmoor as soon as possible. We would love to see you and our grandchildren more often. Joe, write out a check for $4,000.00 dollars, and that is final!"

Elsa embraced her mom and dad, and I gave them a big, warm hug and said, "We are blessed to have so much support, and we will pay the loan back within a year."

We all went to see the models. They were overwhelmed to see the spacious plan we liked. The back yard was plenty large enough for a big swimming pool. We filled out the necessary papers, and in a couple of weeks we moved into our beautiful new house in Rossmoor's prestigious community, with the generous help of Mr. and Mrs. Cash. The move changed our lives. Elsa made friends very quickly, and the children met lots of playmates. Mom got her wish, as she had more chances to baby sit, but we never felt pressure as they left us to live our own lives.

I had no choice but to drive daily from Rossmoor to Eagle Rock, about one hour each way, a small price to pay for the happiness of my family. I hired dad as a cashier for the busy weekends.

About eight months had passed since we had gotten the loan from mom and dad. We had a family dinner at our home and I handed mom and dad a 'Thank You' note with a blank check inside. Dad remarked, "This is a quick repayment, but why did you leave the amount blank? It should be $4,000.00."

I replied, "You're right, the amount was $4,000 but I left the check open to add interest."

Dad jumped to his feet, "Are you kidding me? Do you think we would charge you interest?"

I had to retreat, "It was generous of you to make it possible for us to move into our dream home. I am not used to that kind of human kindness. I didn't mean to offend you, but somehow I felt your generosity was overwhelming and in no way did I want to short change you."

Dad stepped close to me and put his hands on my shoulders, looking straight into my eyes. "Son, you are not talking to strangers, you are part of our family, and you are one of us. We feel like you are our son, you better get used to it. There is no way we can replace your parents, but I'm sure they would do the same if the situations were reversed." We hugged each other, and there wasn't a dry eye in the room.

Raising the Family

The year was 1960 and Daryl began school while Michele started to walk. We noticed she had difficulty walking, as she wobbled a lot. We made an appointment with a specialist, Dr. Frederic Ilfeld. He diagnosed her as having a Congenital Hip. After several consultations, he put her in a brace, called the "Ilfeld Splint". She had to wear it day and night. For us it was heartbreaking to watch the discomfort she had to bear, but young children are resilient and she did get adjusted to walking with the brace. She was walking surprisingly well in an awkward position, with her legs spread wide apart. Many times we got stopped by people who were amazed at how well she walked. Eventually she could sleep without the brace, as she slowly got cured, thanks to Dr. Ilfeld. Michele was always proud that she had been one of the early pioneers to prove the brace worked and thereby help so many that followed.

Daryl liked school, and we lived our lives, making the best of every situation. The restaurant was now well established. On the weekends people were lined up. I heard many comments about the food being good, and that prices were reasonable. Some people were congratulating me, "You have a little gold mine." It looked good for any onlookers. We made some financial headway, but considering the hours we had to put in, it was not much better than getting wages.

We decided to have a swimming pool with a slide and diving board built in the back yard. I also built a barbeque grill, added benches from cement blocks, a large terrazzo covered table, and I custom made a circular bench around it. After I installed a stereo system outside, I was satisfied and considered the plans completed. We celebrated birthday parties, and held get-togethers for all occasions. We and the children had many friends and they felt welcome in our garden setting. Daryl was almost nine years old and Michele had started school. We were proud to see our daughter, giggling and running around the pool, without any trace of her former handicap. She was totally cured.

On Wednesdays we went to Huntington Beach. We spread our blanket on the warm sandy beach, and we swam and played in the surf with the children, keeping an eye on the waves breaking into heavy surf as they crashed on the shore. As I sat there watching my carefree family, I felt very content, as my life had changed from the ashes of the Holocaust to the golden beaches of California. I looked up and gave a silent thanks to God, my best Friend, and smiled at my beloved brother and family. It was a miracle, to have come through it all. I thought of Vera too, as she had a permanent place in my heart, but I didn't let my private thoughts interfere with my life.

Some weekends I brought Daryl with me to the restaurant. I let him wrap potatoes in foil to be baked. He enjoyed spending time with his dad. Occasionally I let him run the speed boat that I had built for him in the hospital. We built kites together, and launched them by running fast, in the nearby park. Michele was always part of our adventures. She adored her older brother, and Daryl was very protective of his little sister. We were one happy family.

A Trust is Broken

Our life was running smoothly, until one day, arriving at work, after having the previous day off, I casually checked the cash register receipts from the previous night when my partner closed the place. I found $50.00 missing. When I confronted him, he had no excuse, he just turned red as a beet. The following day he handed me an envelope with $50.00 in it without a word. He was not a true 50/50 partner. We had both put in an equal amount of money, but I had no idea how much money he had taken that should have been my share. I had all the responsibility when it came to repairs. It was obvious he had taken advantage of my youth. I had no trouble doing whatever helped our business, as I felt I had to do it for the benefit of my family.

Once I had told David, "I don't mind that I put more work into our restaurant, but at least you are honest." I had spoken too soon. I learned the hard way and I knew we had to dissolve the partnership. I put the business up for sale. I handed him the papers we both had to sign and he signed without any questions. Our relationship was strained, but I had to keep our business going to support my family. I lost all of my feelings for the man who was once my partner. The help was not aware of my dilemma. I figured that if I survived my past, this small challenge was not going to stop me. I just did not let it stress me out as that was not my nature. It took three years before we sold the place. We got cash for "The Sizzling Platter", and even though we did not make a fortune, I had a lot to be proud of.

I had started to look for a job before we closed the sale on the restaurant. I decided to change professions, and I got a job with Sun

Life Insurance Co. The Company put me through training, and I studied hard to pass my insurance test, to become licensed by the state. At that point my training program stopped, and I became a fully licensed insurance salesman. I put in all my effort to become successful. To me it was important that I advance and support my family. My earnings started to climb based on my success. Elsa was still working at home doing alterations and she had built up a good clientele in Rossmoor.

One day as I was returning from the office, Elsa handed me a slip of paper with a name and telephone number. She was eager to inform me, "I was talking to one of my costumers about you. She got excited hearing about your rapid advancement with Sun Life. Her son, Mike Fisher, is an executive with Pennsylvanian Life Insurance Co. and they are looking for young talented people in the industry."

I gave him a call and made an appointment to see him. He hired me on the spot. The following day I said good-bye to Sun Life, and I moved into a new office in Long Beach, California and met Mike's partner, Phil Schrotman. The young executives impressed me. They informed me that to further my career I would have to study for an N.A.S.D. security license. I met this challenge, and after studying extensively for weeks, I was ready to take my test. They were very proud of me when I showed up at the office with my license to prove that I had passed the test. I became a Licensed Insurance Executive, qualified to sell the so-called Equity Funding. It was a concept where Life Insurance was combined with Mutual Funds. I worked in their office for over a year and earned their respect. When the main office called me in for an important interview, I got an offer I could not refuse.

I opened my own office in a brand new building, and hired a sales force and licensed them and hired two office girls. We were in business. I have won many awards from Pennsylvania Life and in 1972 they awarded me with membership in their Hall of Fame. I did work many hours, but never neglected my family. We took extensive vacations every summer, took the children on camping trips, and I taught Daryl the skill of fishing. My children became Boy and Girl Scouts which reminded me of my childhood years. I was very proud of my family.

Inviting My Old Friend from Toronto

I had kept in touch with my old buddies from Toronto, and invited my friend, Miki Friedman, to visit us. He flew to Los Angeles, and stayed with us for a week. He enjoyed meeting my family, and we showed him around the touristic places, Disneyland, Knott's Berry Farm, the beaches, and the surrounding landmarks.

We relaxed beside our backyard swimming pool. Miki wanted me to teach him how to snorkel. That was an easy task. I gave him a spare face mask I had. I put mine on and showed him how to simply swim underwater holding his breath. He put his mask on his forehead, and sitting on the side of the pool, with his feet hanging into the water, he remarked, "Pista this is a cinch. I'm a good swimmer. Just watch me. I can hold my breath for a long time." He pulled his mask down over his face and slipped into the water. With powerful strokes he swam to the bottom at the deep end where the water was 9'. He circled around a few times and put his thumb up, to share his enjoyment. He surfaced to get some air, and he slipped under water again.

Elsa said to me, "He should be surfacing soon."

I was watching him as he was still floating face down. I put on my goggles and jumped in, swimming under Miki and looking into his face mask. His eyes were bulging wide open, with no expression, and his mask was covering his mouth and nose. He looked unconscious! I grabbed him by the arm and pushed his face above the water. I tore off his goggles that were choking him. By that time Elsa was anxiously kneeling at the coping of the pool and reaching towards Miki, and between the two of us, we were able to slide him out of the water. I placed his limp body face down.

There was no water draining, but he was still unconscious, so I gave him CPR, and worked on him for at least five minutes. Finally, he showed symptoms of life. I looked up to the sky, exhausted, and thanked God for Miki's life. By now he was breathing on his own. As we pulled him out of the water over the rough coping of the pool, his chest got scratched and bruised. I explained to him what went wrong. "You put your mask too low. Instead of just covering your nose, you covered your mouth also. When you came up for air, you could not breathe, since the goggles covered your mouth also. You slipped below the surface, and we noticed that you were floating underwater face down. That's when I jumped in to investigate."

This vacation almost turned into a disaster. He was glad to be returning to his wife, Ingrid in Toronto. We got a lovely letter of thanks, from both of them. After Miki left, our life resumed its normalcy.

Shattered Memories

I came home one night, and the children were sleeping. Elsa greeted me, and we just talked. I decided to glance at some of my old memories, so I went to the closet to pull out Vera's letter collection. Elsa was watching me and said in a nasty voice, "You will not find that box. I've burned all of your letters."

I was shocked, and could not find words for such a thoughtless, cruel action. I said, "I'm ashamed of you! I lost my family; this was part of my private childhood, and you destroyed it. I can't believe you could be capable of such an act. We have been married for the past fourteen years, raised our family, and you had the gall to threaten our marriage, by wiping out my last childhood memory? Before we started to date, I told you about Vera, and how I felt about her. I wrote to Vera and ended our relationship. The only thing I have kept is the memory of my childhood, and she was part of it. And now you willingly destroyed the little that I had left from my past. You should be ashamed of yourself. At least you should have had the courtesy to discuss this with me. You have seriously damaged my respect and trust in you."

Her sarcastic grin quickly disappeared and turned into desperate tears and panic.

"I did not want to hurt you; I just wanted those letters out of the way. I did not know how much they meant to you." She tried to get her words out while sobbing.

"You were jealous over an innocent relationship, which was the best memory of my tragic childhood. You had no right to undermine our marriage, and the future of our children. You made a foolish decision." I was still shaken, but I tried to think logically, and do what was the best for the children.

Elsa begged, "I love you, I know it was foolish of me to think of those letters as a threat and not respect them as part of your childhood memories. I beg you, please forgive me?" She was crying uncontrollably, kneeling on the floor, and clutching my knees.

I said, "Let's calm down; we don't want to wake up the children, do we? The damage has been done and cannot be reversed. It will stay between us. Let's continue with our lives, and hope time will ease the damage."

Our lives continued, but we grew a little distant. It was not noticeable from the outside, but within me, I did feel violated. I never brought up the incident again.

Eleven

Becoming A Real Estate Agent

I saw an opportunity in the real estate market. We sold our house in Rossmoor, with all of the furniture, and bought a beautiful two story, new house in Anaheim Hills, California. Of course the children changed schools, and we made new friends. Mom and dad stayed in their comfortable condominium, and we visited each other frequently.

Daryl decided to try his luck in Alaska and he bought an old van. I helped him winterize it, and between the two of us, we transformed it into a miniature motor home. He was eager to start on his adventure. After several days, we got word from him; he sounded enthused and proud to be on his own, independent. It didn't take Daryl too long to land a job at a local Alaskan bar as a bouncer–he was 6'5", a healthy young man. He soon established himself and found an apartment.

Back in Los Angeles, Elsa and I found a good opportunity to buy a small condominium for Daryl. We put a down payment on it, so he would be assured of a place to live after his return. After some time, when he returned, he was very thankful for the condo. He moved in and happily gave us back the down payment. Daryl resumed his life and started dating. Eventually he began dating a girl named Patty Leason, and after dating for awhile, they got married. The ceremony was at her parents' house. It was a nice occasion, and we were very happy for them. With a little luck our family name could be kept alive.

The stock market turned to a downside trend. I had to approach several of my costumers and I had to make a margin call, to save their insurance from being cancelled. This was not the intent when I got into management, so I made a decision and studied to get my real estate license.

Elsa greeted me one day when I came back from my office, "Pista, congratulations!" She was waving this large official envelope. "I could not wait so I opened it. You have your real estate license." She gave me a big hug as we went in the house and celebrated with a cocktail. I kept my Insurance office going, and no one knew my intentions, except my family. I was negotiating with Viron Realty, who was willing to hire me as a salesman. I made an appointment with Burt Borman, a top executive of Pennsylvania Life, and handed him my resignation. He was sorry to see me go. That was not his wish, but it was my choice.

The new company appreciated my work habits and rapidly accelerating sales. I got promoted to manager in the Orange office. It was located on Katella Ave. in a strip mall. I ran a successful office, and earned the trust of my sales staff. I won many trophies during sales' competitions.

We decided to put our house up for sale in Anaheim Hills, and within a couple of weeks, we sold it for a good profit. Not much later, we bought another new house. We were lucky to vacate one house and move right into another in the same area. We only stayed a year to avoid paying capital gain taxes. We moved again, selling the house, and making a few more dollars, and then we bought two new homes side by side with a view overlooking Anaheim Hills. We moved into one house and rented the other. I contracted to build a large, unusually shaped Jacuzzi, of my own design. It was shaped like a club on a playing card. We lived there almost one year. Our tenants decided to buy the rental they lived in.

Coping with Life

Time flew by. I had had my Real Estate Office for over nine years. I noticed that lately Elsa's behavior had changed, since we bought into Anaheim Hills. Some days she was late coming home with just excuses instead of explanations.

We got some bad news; Michele had developed a problem and discomfort with her legs, and sometimes she had difficulty walking. We took her to doctors, and she underwent thorough examinations, without any concrete results.

None of my jobs had offered me any retirement benefits. One of my part time sales' representatives, who was an appliance salesman at Sears, told me about the good working conditions, and their retirement program. It gave me an idea to better my prospects for retirement, so my attention became focused on Sears. Before giving up my real estate office, I applied to Sear's for a position in their appliance division. The human relation's office informed me that no jobs were available. I didn't settle for a NO answer. I insisted and got an appointment with the store manager. When I entered his office, he was sitting behind a large, highly polished desk. He offered me a seat and asked me, "You have been told no jobs are available, so what can I do for you?"

My answer came without any hesitation, "Sir, I have been managing several offices in the past few years. I'm hoping to get a job with your corporation for an extended period of time. Your corporation is noted for fairness, and offering good retirement plans to people who earn and deserve them. I was told you have no openings as an appliance salesman, but I would take any position you might have."

"That is correct, but I do have an opening in the decorating department. Do you have any knowledge in that field?" he asked.

"No, I have not, but let me make a promise, there is no obstacle or job offered to me, that I cannot handle, and excel in doing it. You give me a chance, and by the end of the year I will be your top producer," I challenged him.

He looked surprised. "My, what confidence! Tell me a little bit about your background."

I got into some of my background and he said, "You have been through hell. Just for you to be here, is a miracle. You are hired." He shook my hand, and said, "Welcome to Sears, it is my privilege to have you." They scheduled me for extensive training. Of course I gave my notice at Viron Realty.

Going Our Separate Ways

In addition to Michele's medical difficulties, Elsa announced she wanted out of our marriage. She had fallen in love with someone else, so I agreed to a divorce. My major concern was Michele's health. We did go through with the divorce, and there were no emotional outbursts. The ones who got hurt the most were Elsa's mom and dad. They were furious with Elsa. I reassured them that my relationship with them would not change. I respected them as if they were parents to me.

After our divorce Elsa moved out and Michele and I stayed in our home in Anaheim Hills. Michele was working at Palm Harbor Hospital as a radiology technician. Daily she drove to work. One morning, she called to me from her bedroom, "Dad, I need your help."

I rushed in to see her. She was sitting on her bed getting ready to go to work, but was having difficulty putting on her stockings. Of course I helped her. "Are you O.K. to go to work?" I asked.

She told me that she was fine; she just had trouble lifting her legs to put on the stockings. I made our usual breakfast, toast and coffee, with jam and cheese. She was ready to leave for work, and reassured me that she was fine. I watched her driving off. I waited for several seconds, and then jumped in my car and followed her, leaving enough distance between us, to not make it obvious. I was relieved when she parked her car in the hospital's parking lot. I was very concerned. My divorce had affected me somewhat, but not enough to really upset me. Since Elsa had burned my childhood memories with Vera, there was emptiness in my heart toward her.

When I came home from the office that same day, I was relieved when I saw Michele's car in the driveway. She was happy to tell me that one of the specialists, a neurologist at Palm Harbor Hospital, noticed her difficulty in walking, and recommended taking a biopsy from her leg. She was officially an adult, but she wanted our advice. I contacted Elsa and we both agreed.

Since the divorce I had listed our house on the market, and it didn't take long to find a buyer. We got a good offer and accepted it. As soon as the house was sold, I looked and found a brand new, very nice, two story condominium, with a small, private back garden. I bought it and we moved in after we left Anaheim Hills. The buyers of our house were friendly people, an American husband, Ed and Lisa, a German war bride. All the papers were signed, and they stopped by to inspect the house. The wife was very talkative and she asked me bluntly, "Mr. Nasser, I know you have been divorced for a while. Would you be interested in meeting a nice young lady? A good friend of mine has been a widow for several years. She is a registered nurse. I can give her a call, would you talk to her? You would make a nice couple."

I thought for a minute. "Sure go ahead, the phone is on the desk."

She dialed, said a few words on the phone, and then she turned to me, "Here, she is on the line, her name is Françoise, she is French Canadian."

I talked to Françoise for almost half an hour, and arranged to meet her. When we met we decided to see each other again, and we started dating. We both felt very comfortable in each other's company. I introduced her to Michele, and later to Daryl, and we became really good friends.

Michele had her leg biopsy, and she was diagnosed with Myasthenia Gravis (MG), an autoimmune disorder where the signal from the nerves to the muscles is blocked, and the muscles become increasingly weaker over time, eventually leading to death unless the progression could be stopped by medication, a thymectomy or both. The medication and the removal of the thymus gland may reverse, stop, slow, or have no effect, depending on the patient.

She needed immediate surgery, and was admitted to U.C.L.A. where the surgery took place. During that time she was dating a young man,

Cecil "Paul" Jones. He took the news in stride, and remained committed to Michele, despite her medical problems.

As Elsa and I had not seen each other for a while, we agreed to visit Michele in the hospital. We waited in the recovery room where our only conversation was about our daughter. Elsa thanked me for taking care of Michele. After a long wait, we were finally allowed to see her. She was taken to an ICU room, where she was still groggy, but able to squeeze our hands, which felt reassuring. We consulted the doctor, and he informed us that the operation was a success, and with good care, Michele might leave the hospital in a couple of weeks.

Elsa and I arranged to meet the following morning. We both arrived at the same time, and we were shocked to see the empty bed with the mattress turned over. The charge nurse came running in, seeing us in shock. "Mr. and Mrs. Nasser, Michele has been transferred from ICU to a regular ward. She is doing very well." We had expected the worst. Thank God she was recovering very rapidly. We talked to her, and she talked about returning to work. It was a great relief.

The following morning I drove Françoise to see Michele. They had a very friendly conversation. Michele did not mind when Françoise gave her a kiss on the cheek for good luck. After a few days, Michele was discharged from the hospital and I took her back home. Michele miraculously returned to work in a week. I thank God that Michele's MG had stabilized but still would require her to take daily medication for the rest of her life, and although the medication was always accompanied by nausea, at least she could otherwise live a full life. She was the type of person who never complained.

Paul asked us for our permission to marry Michele, and we were overwhelmed. He stayed committed to Michele despite her sickness. My admiration for Paul will remain as long as I live. The marriage took place in 1979. We decided that Elsa and I would be at the wedding with the rest of our family. We were her parents, even though I had no emotional feelings left toward Elsa.

Twelve

Starting a New Life

François and I got engaged, and Elsa remarried in February, 1981. Françoise and I set our big date for April 5th, 1981. We got married in Laguna Beach, California, with Michele and Daryl, and Mr. and Mrs. Deighton, Françoise's parents, attending the ceremony.

Françoise and Stephen's wedding with her parents, Mr. and Mrs. Deighton..

We spent our honeymoon in Tahiti, and had a major reception in Anaheim after we returned. Many friends and relatives attended our reception. (Daryl and Patti had bought a house in Corona. Their daughter, Andrea, was born in April 1981, so Patty could not attend our wedding reception.)

Our new home in Yorba Linda, was only a couple of miles from my previous home in Anaheim Hills. Françoise had a fully furnished condo in Placentia. She rented her condo, and we moved into our new place. She and I had lots of fun furnishing our home. I was still working for Sears as a decorator, and made many house calls. I learned quickly and soon earned the respect of my superiors. As a registered nurse, Françoise's private duty kept her working during the nights. My appointments had no time frame; I had to go to homes, whenever they had time to receive me. In the mornings when I got up, and was ready to leave for work, Francoise came back from a 12 hour shift. Our bed was hardly empty, which created a challenge.

We installed an eight person, octagon Jacuzzi in the back yard and built a gazebo around it. We enjoyed it and used it a lot, having Michele, Daryl, and their spouses over for family gatherings. In 1982, Daryl and his family moved to Oak Grove, Missouri. The same year we got some great news; Patti was expecting again. She gave birth to Andrew in 1983 on August 11th, and a few months later, Michele had a daughter, Chelsea, who was born on Dec. 27th. Michele and Paul bought a house, where they comfortably settled. Françoise was hired by St. Jude's Hospital as a chemical dependency nurse. She liked her new position, but she still worked night shifts.

We both liked camping, so we bought a nice sized tent, and spent many weekends driving to nearby mountains and campgrounds, enjoying nature and each other's company.

Françoise had downhill skiing experience, while I had done only a little cross country skiing. To please me, she sold all of her downhill equipment, and switched to cross-country skiing. For years to follow, we skied at different ski resorts,

Francoise and Stephen camping

starting locally in the St. Bernardino Mountains. As I improved, we ventured to Mammoth, June Lake, Lake Tahoe and Sun Valley in California. For me, cross-country skiing sometimes became difficult, following in the pre-grooved tracks, especially when they iced up. Later in June Lake, I learned downhill skiing. I took lessons for my safety, and I quickly learned the correct way. From then on, we had many enjoyable skiing vacations.

Francoise and Stephen skiing.

Barbara and Mike have joined us on several occasions. We have also stayed with them during a skiing vacation we took in Wolf Springs, Colorado.

Françoise and I bought two bicycles, which we used very often. Occasionally we rode in a nearby riverbed all the way to the beach. It was over ten miles each way. We also played tennis a lot, with our good friends, Marylynn and Creed. In 1984 we bought a time-share in Laguna, right on the beach. We enjoyed many memorable summer vacations.

Trip to Budapest

Françoise and I planned to visit the few family members remaining in Budapest, Hungary. I still had my Uncle Charles and his wife, Ilonka. One night we had dinner at their place, but we stayed in a hotel, as they lived in a tiny condo. Uncle Charles had a heart of gold. I never told him about my diary that I had written in the Concentration Camp. As long as he lived, I kept it a secret. He must not find out the details about how his wife, Aunt Bozsi and baby, Peter were murdered in front of my eyes.

I showed Françoise the city, and the house I used to live in on Arpad Street, and also the Gymnasium, a school where I had studied with my brother. We rented a car and drove through some parts of Hungary that neither she nor I had ever seen. We visited Lake Balaton, one of the largest lakes in Europe. I showed Françoise the place where I used to vacation with my parents, and the "jetty" Andris and I had fished from in Balaton, Boglar. Memories of good old times rushed through my mind.

Andris and Pista, fishing at Lake Balaton, 1942.

Then we drove on, stopping by several communities, seeing the local sights. At the end of one day we dined in a "Csarda" specializing in native Hungarian cuisine, like "Gulyas". The Gypsy musicians brought tears to my eyes, bringing back memories of olden times. We ended up in Budapest, where we wined and dined to our pleasure. Then we spent a couple of days at my cousin, Daisy's apartment, who lives close to the Royal castle. We also met my cousin, Dr. Veres Pal and his wife, Ana. Flying back from Budapest, we stopped at Francoise's family in Montreal, Canada Like all holidays, it came to an end, and we returned home to the USA.

Bringing Charles and Helen to Los Angeles

We arranged and brought Uncle Charles and his wife to California. It was a very happy occasion! They stayed with us in Yorba Linda for about a month. I had to be careful to hide my manuscript, written in the Camp as a diary, from Uncle Charles, as it held all the details of his wife, Bozsi's, and child, Peter's, murders that I had eye-witnessed. Before his arrival I hid all the papers related to my diary in the attic.

We drove Helen and Uncle Charles to Palm Springs and Disneyland and showed them all the sights we could. We took a few days to stay in Las Vegas, which was one of their highlights. There, we ordered a newspaper with their name in the headlines: "Ilonka es Karoly (Charles and Helen) Gets Rich in Las Vegas"!

Charles and Helen in Las Vegas.

They were anxious to take the paper home to Budapest, and fool their friends. I'm sure they both had the time of their lives! Before we knew it, it was time for us to say good-bye, and they returned to Budapest.

That same year, we coaxed Mr. and Mrs. Deighton, Francoise's parents, to visit us in California. We also took them on their first cruise to Hawaii, for their 50th Anniversary.

Moving to Nevada

Our Toyota Motor Home, 1993.

In 1992, we started to plan our retirement for the years to follow. We wanted to travel coast to coast across the U.S. and Canada. Francoise and I decided that a small motor home would make our trip possible. I wanted to have a self-contained unit that Françoise and I could drive. During our search, we found just the right size, and made a quick decision to buy a six cylinder, 21' Toyota Motor Home.

I convinced Françoise to drive it around, and she handled it very well, so we bought it and drove it home. We had friends, Cliff and Karen, who owned a large property in Chino, a few miles away from our house, and they were nice enough to let us keep the vehicle there until we were retired.

In 1993, we put our house up for sale as we planned to build a home in Las Vegas. We bought brand new bedroom, living, and dining room furniture in Upland, California with the agreement that the furniture would be held and delivered after our new home was built. Our house in Yorba Linda was sold in a short time. Sadly, Francoise received a call from Montreal; her dad was seriously ill, and she had to fly back to Montreal. I had to stay behind to take care of all the paperwork, then pack and move. It was a sad occasion when I got a call from Françoise, telling me the bad news that her father had passed away.

After Françoise returned back home, we made our move to Las Vegas. I drove the motor home and Françoise followed me in the car with the movers behind us. We placed all our belongings in rented storage and went to our future home site in Los Prados, Nevada, with a realtor, who had taken us there on a previous occasion. We bought the house, and it was contracted to be built by December, 1993. Los Prados was a gated community and had a place to park the motor home.

With all of the paperwork signed, for our future residence and all the arrangements made, we were in a unique situation. We had no expenses to pay, such as a mortgage, or electricity, telephone, water, etc. We left our car in the secured, gated parking facility in Los Prados, and equipped our new motor home with a generator, TV and VCR. It became our home on wheels, until December, when our new home that was being built would be ready for us to move into. In the meantime, we traveled around the United States. It was a new, but enjoyable experience. Our motor home was only 21', so we were able to fit in most parking spaces. We stopped at several campgrounds, and hooked up to services. No matter where we stopped, we were home.

Front top left: Daryl and Patty,
Paul and Michele, Rose,,

Andrea, Andrew, Stephen,
Francoise and Chelsea.

First, we drove to Oak Grove, Missouri to visit Daryl and his family. We were surprised at how the children had grown; Andrea was 11 and Andrew was now 9. Daryl was working for the fire department, and they had bought a house. On the weekends, we drove the grandchildren to a couple of caves and spent some family time, driving around. We could not keep them too long, as they had school to attend.

After spending time with family in Oak Grove, we headed to Branson, Missouri. Branson has many well-known entertainers: western singers, musicians, and violinists performing in their own auditoriums. We hooked up the motor home in a campground, and saw many of the excellent shows. Enjoying the privilege of being retired with no timetables to follow, we drove through several states and many cities, and headed to St. Louis to visit friends. We toured the architectural marvel, the St. Louis Arch, as we crossed the mighty Mississippi River. It was enjoyable driving, and sightseeing.

Next, heading north towards western Canada, we got on the Trans-Canadian Highway and drove west toward Manitoba. We were making good time until the road changed; the super highway ended. Travelling through some flat country of Saskatchewan, we stopped by campgrounds to rest overnight. Our Toyota held up well; we only had one flat tire. Eventually we arrived in Alberta at the foothills of the Rocky Mountains. Banff was surrounded by majestic peaks near beautiful Lake Louise. It is a breathtaking sight! There we camped in a well-located facility, did some shopping and bought some souvenirs. Also we enjoyed swimming in the pool, and making a mini-vacation out of it. We hiked beside the lake, and left the shimmering waters below us as we gained altitude. Finally, we reached a Japanese teahouse, and had our refreshments sitting on the outside patio, admiring the breath-taking panorama. As we continued our adventure, following the road, each time we came to a curve, some unexpected marvel of nature came into view. Eventually we descended, leaving the mountain region behind.

We arrived at the great city of Vancouver, and continued our travel to British Columbia. A few days later we drove onto a ferry boat; our destination was Salt Spring Island, where Françoise's cousin, June, and her husband, Phil, lived. They had retired in this lovely place. Than we hopped over to Victoria and visited Bouchard Gardens, the nicest botanical gardens we have seen. The huge flower clock at the entrance stole the show. At the Empress Hotel, we ordered an elegant English High Tea. We hiked around the Island, and a few days later took the ferry back to the mainland.

On the way back to the U.S., we stopped in San Francisco, and spent several more days, visiting interesting sights the city has to offer. Of course, we had to ride their famous trolley street cars and we had fun helping at the last station, when everybody got off and turned the car around so it could go back to where it came from. We couldn't stay too long as we had to get back home. At the end of the trip, we planned to park our motor home in Los Prados, and check the progress of our new house under construction. The building was progressing according to schedule.

Thirteen

After we arranged all of the paperwork and our plans were final-
ized, Françoise and I were ready for a European vacation, knowing
we had to be back in December to move into our brand new home.
We arranged to pick up a car in Holland, got the car without any difficulty, and drove to Paris, France. I had some memories from 1948 as
a 16-year-old young man when I had immigrated to Canada. This time
I was 62 years old and married, and it was enjoyable sharing the trip
with my wife. She spoke excellent French; it helped a lot to be able to
communicate easily. I was surprised, especially in Paris, when she had
a conversation with a native, who snubbed her by saying, "Oh, you are
French Canadian."

Back in the U.S., I had been given the Parisian address of a distant
relative, Dr. Michael Spector. We met them and had dinner in their
house. He did agree that some people are snobbish, but he said that we
would find people much friendlier outside the city, and he was right.

We had to cover a lot of sights, so we drove on to Monaco and visited
the lavish museum. I was curious and got information about the Royal
family. Our next stop was Monte Carlo, and its elegant casino. We curiously looked in just to get an idea if it lived up to its fame, because we did

not gamble. In the South of France we drove to the walled city of St. Paul De Vince, leaving the car outside the city gate as no cars were allowed there. We did a lot of walking in this picturesque, charming place, and felt like we had stepped into another century. In a little shop, we met a local artist and admired his unique creations of dried flowers displayed on rice paper, like paintings. We bought four of them for our kitchen. Afterwards, we explored the walls surrounding the city. We knew in our hearts that one day we would have to come back to re-visit this hidden gem.

We continued driving to Germany and visited Muhldorf, my former Concentration Camp. I relied on my limited amount of knowledge of the German language, and adding our English and French together, we had no problem communicating. It was emotional to trace my steps back to 1944/45, as I visited the mass grave, where I suspected my brother might be buried. I left the site with haunting memories. I usually have no problem falling asleep, but tonight it was different. I had horrible nightmares. Andris laid defenseless on the ground, as this Nazi bully, was ready to smash my brother's head with a heavy metal object. I rushed to stop the blow, and I screamed!

I awoke as Françoise shook me, "Pista, it's OK. It's OK. You must have had a bad dream." She was trying to comfort me.

I snapped back to reality, and replied, "It was so real, just like when it happened many years ago. I'm fine now." I tried to reassure her.

Next, we drove to Garmisch, a jewel in Bavaria, and found a pension in a typical Bavarian home that looked like it had popped straight out of a storybook. We stayed a few days, and covered the neighboring country-side. We kept on driving to Salzburg, which was like stepping into a history book; the birthplace of Mozart, and other musicians of yester-year. Above the city on top of the hill was a Castle so we took time out to explore it. The view was breath-taking! We enjoyed the Bavarian food, especially the Wiener schnitzel, and dined and wined in Beer Gardens where locals gathered.

We crossed into Switzerland, and to save some high altitude mountain driving, put the car on a train, staying in the car as we went through the

St. Gothard Tunnel. It was an exciting experience. Zurich was next, where we spent a few days, and found lodging at the nearest hotel to the railroad station. We were eager to see the Matterhorn. The village of Zermatt was our next destination, but as no cars were allowed in Zermatt, the only way to get there was by train. All visitors had to park their cars at the railroad station, many miles away from our destination. At the station there was a display board of hotels available in Zermatt and each listed a telephone connection. I made several enquiries, and then made a reservation. We boarded the train and by the time we arrived, it was dark. Disembarking, we found ourselves in the middle of a fairy tale setting of twinkling lights of homes and hotels built in the Bavarian style. Through their windows, the lights gave a charming glow to the small village. Our hotel was nearby, and after checking in we were ushered to an old fashioned, but comfortable room. Shutters on the windows gave us total privacy. That night we had a typical Swiss fondue dinner, in their cozy restaurant. After dinner, we could hardly wait to climb under the feather-puffed eiderdowns.

We must have been exhausted, as morning came very quickly. The clanging sound of church bells woke us up. Françoise was behind me looking over my shoulder as I opened the shutter. The breath-taking scenery overwhelmed our eyes. Not too far in the distance, we saw the Matterhorn. It was a majestic view! Totally covered by snow, it looked like an artificial cream puff. In the foreground, the village of Zermatt stretched to the snow-covered slopes, partially hidden by a misty cloud. Not far from our hotel, a church with its single spire was in view and that's where the sound of bells came from. We just hugged each other, as we were overwhelmed and eager to start our day. Within walking distance from the hotel was an electric train service to a high snow-covered plateau overlooking the magnificent peeks of the Swiss Alps. We had fun admiring the frigid landscape even though we were not properly dressed for the blasts of cold air, blowing hard from the icy glacier. Later, we returned to the village, and found an outdoor coffee shop where we ordered two mugs of Swiss hot chocolate. We took lots of pictures, enjoying the Matterhorn and spending two days exploring Zermatt.

After our stay there, we took the train back, and drove to Zurich, staying in the Lake District. While window-shopping, we came across this fancy cuckoo clock, and we both fell in love with it and bought it on the spot. Afterward, we headed to Geneva, the international city, overlooking the lake with the same name. Again, we visited many sights.

Our adventure continued into Italy as we drove along many country roads. We enjoyed wine tasting and touring the centuries-old facilities. In Pisa, we took a lot of pictures of the Leaning Tower. It is amazing, as it has defied gravity for such a long time.

Whenever we wanted to stop for the night, we just drove to the railroad station where we always found a list of pensions that we could choose from and stay in. This way of traveling created an adventure and a challenge. Arriving in Rome was an experience, as traffic was very congested. They drove like maniacs! We found a centrally located hotel not too far from the Vatican. It took us two days to partially visit the Holy City, taking many photos of the famous, "Swiss Guards". We stopped by Trevy Fountain with its cascading waters around the magnificent sculptures. There is a tradition at the fountain, and we followed it, tossing three coins in the water over our shoulders. Next on our must-see list, was the ancient Coliseum. We didn't need much imagination to hear the cheering of the crowd, the clashing swords of the gladiators, and the roar of the lions.

After a good night's rest we continued our adventures and arrived in Naples. We were interested in seeing Pompeii. At the hotel they warned us to be extra careful of the motorized thieves, hoodlums driving their mopeds and ripping off the shoulder handbags of unsuspecting pedestrians. We got to Pompeii, the old Roman city that was covered by volcanic ashes after the sudden eruption of Mount Vesuvius. During the excavations, up to 15 feet of ashes had to be removed. We saw colorful frescoes remaining on partially standing walls of villas that had once belonged to nobility. We walked on the original narrow streets paved by hand-hewn stones. There were visible impressions left by the wheels of chariots, created many centuries ago. In the museum, we were amazed to view the cast plaster impressions, of figures with distorted facial expression, suffocated from the erupting volcanoes poisonous gasses, and covered by the falling ashes. We were fascinated by our adventures. We took full advantage of our early retirement. I was 62 years of age and Françoise 54. We had no responsibilities, except to each other.

From Pompeii, we stopped in many smaller communities, watching for 'Pension for Rent' signs usually displayed in windows. Finally, we approached Venice where we had a very difficult time locating a room for rent. Tourists were everywhere, and I was desperate, but determined. Temporarily parking the car with Françoise behind the wheel, I disappeared into the crowd beside the local boat terminal. Keeping my eyes and ears open, luck was on my side. An English-speaking, Italian gentleman stopped me, asking, "Are you looking for accommodations? It is almost impossible to find any. If you don't mind traveling about 15 minutes by water taxi, I do own a house, and have a room with a bath room, for two people."

My eyes lit up for a second, and then I said, "It would be great, but we are driving, I left my wife in the car."

He smiled. "No problem. We will put your car on a ferry; I will go with you, and you can drive me to the house. Your car will be safe in my gated property. To get around and go to Venice, we have regular boat service like city buses. They run all day frequently."

I had no other choice, so we agreed on a fair price. We walked back to Françoise, switched drivers, and followed his plan. It worked like a charm, just as he had described it. We had a comfortable room for the next few days, and we got adjusted to the boat transportation. We made connections to several small islands, including Murano, where the world-famous glass factory is located. In Venice, we spent several days sightseeing; St. Mark's Square was awesome as we walked over the typical Venetian bridges. Some had lots of local handicrafts offered for sale by eager vendors. We used many rolls of films and did some shopping, and dined in charming typical Italian eateries.

One particular morning we took our boat to St. Mark's Square. Because of the high tide, there was some water as we approached the

Square. It was not flooded, but obviously we had to be careful. We saw several eateries and shops and heard the sound of an orchestra coming from a two-storied Café Shop. Several tourists were coming out; we conversed with a couple, and asked them about the food inside this cafe. They informed us that the food and pastries were excellent. They also said that when we go inside, we will notice an orchestra playing on their balcony. Make sure the waiter takes your order when the orchestra is not playing, that way you will be charged around $2.50 in American money for your coffee. If he takes your order after the music starts, you will pay $5.00 a cup. What the couple had told us was correct. The pastries we had were mouth watering, but we only paid $2.50 per cup of coffee, and still enjoyed the music.

It was time to leave, and we drove again towards the West, Françoise and I alternating driving to make it easier on both of us. We arrived in the beautiful city of Florence, the home of Michelangelo's masterpiece, "David". We went into the museum and admired the statue, studying it from all angles.

Françoise and I wanted to complete our Hungarian Herend china collection. We were advised that Florence was the best place to find that particular china. We were successful, and placed a large order to be delivered to our new home address in Las Vegas sometime in 1994. We walked the streets, and walked over Florence's well-known bridge loaded with vendors on both sides.

We had a long drive ahead of us, so after studying the maps, we took different routes. In Belgium, we stopped at Antwerp, the headquarters of the diamond cutting industry and visited a workshop. It was interesting to me as a former diamond setter. We drove back to Holland and dropped off our rented car. Our extended European vacation came to an end, as we returned to Las Vegas with good memories and lots of pictures. We were both very anxious to move into our new house.

Fourteen

Los Prados 1993

It was December, 1993 when we got the keys to our new house. We were very pleased!

I unlocked the door, and ceremoniously I picked up Françoise, and carried her into our home. Of course the house was empty; the carpeting had to be installed the following day, and the new furniture would be delivered from Upland, California a few days later. We parked the motor home in front of the house and slept there comfortably until our furniture was delivered. Finally we were all set, and it was a pleasure to sleep in our own bed in our own home. We had hardly moved in, and I was anxious to hang the four pictures on the kitchen wall that we had purchased in St. Paul De Vince. We celebrated Chanukah, Christmas, and New Year's in our new home.

Our gated golf community, Los Prados, had several amenities: a large club house and restaurant, rooms to accommodate card players, or social gatherings, a library, and changing rooms with lockers, for golfers or swimmers. It also had two swimming pools and Jacuzzis, and two tennis courts. We played tennis whenever we had a chance and walked around Los Prados Circle, a walk of about 45 minutes. We also cycled within our community. During the warm season we used our motor home a lot, feeling like modern "Gypsies". In the wintertime we took our skiing gear and headed to ski resorts in Utah, Colorado, and California. In between we hiked a lot in our local mountains of Mount Charleston and Spring Mountain. We also camped out in Death Valley, California, and in Valley of the Fire, Nevada. We kept very active meeting many nice people and kept our connections with couples we met during our travels. Our social calendar kept us very busy. We joined a Bridge Club, and made time to play duplicate bridge. We also played a friendly game "Pan" with some nice couples we have met.

I had another project in mind, as I loved to build self-designed models of ships, buildings, and airplanes. When Daryl was small I had started to build him a model railroad. I enjoyed watching him playing with his "Choo-Choo Train". Of course it got broken, and with time he lost interest. Now that I was retired, I decided to build a large H.O. model train layout. In the garage I started to build a table with folding legs, 4' X 8 1/2' in size. It was a challenge to move it into a spare room. I meticulously designed the layout of the tracks and elevated the figure eight with an over-crossing and a large oval circle at the base, with switches, to make it functional. Then I worked on the terrain, creating mountain peaks, waterfalls, a lake, a ski lift and slope, and a steaming volcano. I also included a desert section with cactus, an Indian enclave with mud huts, grazing cattle, and Indian ponies, a city section with an old-fashioned hotel and a movie theater, a school house, and two railway stations. I fashioned the mountains from wire mesh supported by wooden sticks for rigidity. I created eight tunnels leading through formulated rock formations. Then came the big challenge. The framework of the wire skeleton of the mountains and the lay-out was taking shape. To make it look real, I had to make the mountains, forests, lake, and the rest look realistic. I did not follow books or instructions. No paper-mâché for me! I experimented with cement powder, plaster of Paris, and grout in different colors.

Eventually, I got the right mixture and texture and I applied it with a brush covering every square inch of the layout. I waited a full day before reapplying the next coat. Ultimately, I added eight coats which

The railroad Pista Built, with family portrait he painted.

took over a week, and I was very pleased with the finished product. I bought a bag full of artificial grass, and sprinkled it on a quick-drying, gluey base. I used the same method for the red, beige, and earth-colored sand I collected from the desert. It took me 600 hours to complete my project!

Trip to the Bahamas, 1994

Françoise and I flew to the Bahamas taking our snorkeling gear with us. The place is an underwater paradise; no wonder it is called Paradise Island! We checked into our hotel and set out to explore the surrounding community. We had lunch in a charming restaurant named "Papillion". The following day we went snorkeling off a sugar white sandy beach. We put on our fins, goggles and swim jackets and entered the warm, clear turquoise water. Suddenly, Françoise squeezed my hand several times. I looked in the direction she pointed, and there was a school of colorful tropical fish. We headed towards them, but they scattered in all directions. We must have spent well over an hour enjoying this living aquarium. After changing back to our clothing, we were starved and had a great meal at the "Papillion Restaurant". Back at the hotel, we relaxed on the patio with tropical drinks.

I had my Schaffhausen gold watch on my wrist, the same watch I brought with me when I immigrated to Canada in 1948. It was working well, but the crown of the winding mechanism was worn very thin. I was afraid it might break off because I had to wind the watch daily. I asked at the hotel registration if they knew a good watchmaker, and they gave me the address of a jewelry shop. I set out to find the place, located in a small shopping area. As I entered the small store, a watchmaker was sitting behind his work bench. He must have been at least 15 years older than I.

He stood up and lifted his magnifying glasses to his forehead, and greeted me in accented English, "Can I help you?"

I answered, "I hope you can." I took off my watch and showed it to him. "I bought this watch from our jewelry store many years ago, and I am afraid to wind it, because the crown looks very fragile."

He took the watch and with amazement, exclaimed, "This is a genuine Schaffhausen!" Then he continued, "You have an accent, where are you from?"

"I'm from Budapest, Hungary."

He quickly replied, extending his hand to shake mine, "That's amazing! I'm Hungarian also! In what part of Budapest was your store?"

"It was in the outskirts, called Ujpest," I replied.

He looked at me closely, and said, "In Ujpest, there was only one store that would have carried such an expensive watch–the Nasser Jewelers."

Now I was amazed. "How do you know the Nasser?!" I exclaimed.

"I once worked in their store as a watch repair man."

I burst out, "Are you Tony?" I asked him in amazement.

"Yes, that is my name!" He had tears in his eyes. Are you little Robi?" *

We embraced. Finally we let go and just looked at each other. Tony continued,

"When I left your store in 1937, you were just a little boy. How is your father, Dezso, your mother, Georgie, and you had an older brother, Andris, and your Uncle Charles?"

I looked straight in his eyes and informed him, "Uncle Charles is still living in Budapest, but all the others have been murdered in the Holocaust. I'm the only one who survived."

Tony cried out, "Those gangsters!" He tightly embraced me and we sobbed on each others' shoulders. He pulled up a chair, and I had to tell him the sad facts of the past. He fixed my watch and would not take any money. I did give him information about how to get in touch with Uncle Charles. They communicated until 1996, when my uncle passed away.

*My name at birth was Nasser Robert Istvan. Everyone called me Robi. When I was around 8 years old, at school people nicknamed me "Bobbi", a favored name for pet dogs. Than they carried my nickname further, and called me, "Here Bobbi, here boy", and whistled for me to go to them. I asked my parents if it would be OK if I used my second given name Istvan. They thought it was a good idea, to minimize my embarrassment. Istvan was a very popular name in Hungary. Most Istvans were called "Pista', an accepted nickname. When you hear "Pista", it is just a popular substitute for Istvan. In English, my name is Stephen "Pista" Nasser.

Invitation to Germany 1995

In late 1994 I received a letter from Germany. When I opened the envelope, I could hardly believe my eyes! The letter stated that according to their information, I was liberated on April 30, 1945 by General Patton's Third Army. They requested a reply, if my name was Istvan (Stephen) Nasser, and if I was on the so-called "Death Train". The organization invited me to attend their April 30th celebration of the 50th Year of the Liberation, in Seeshaupt, Germany, arriving on April 28th and staying till May 5th. They would cover most expenses, and we would stay with a German family.

I happily accepted the invitation, and flew to Seeshaupt with Françoise. We were warmly welcomed with a reception. As soon as we were settled in our landlady's comfortable house, we were treated to a delicious home-cooked dinner. During the dinner conversation we found out that our hosts had fled during the 1940's to Switzerland to escape the Nazi terror. They were Christian people. After the war, upon their return, they reclaimed their house, and fixed it up so it was livable again.

The next day we attended a well-planned reception followed by a full dinner. Each one of us was given a copy of a German newspaper, showing the picture taken by a photo journalist on April 30, 1945, of the liberated "Death Train", with 64 bodies lying at all angles. There were many people and city officials attending. We survivors numbered about 25, the remaining few, lucky to be alive after Muhldorf's Hard Labor Camp.

The following day, on April 30th, we all attended a ceremony. After the speeches came the unveiling of the Memorial by the artist. It was created from metal salvaged from railroad and train parts, and was about 10' tall, an impressive square tower.

We had a few days before we would be returning to the U.S., so our host wanted to show us the community and drive us around. She asked me if I remembered the hospital I was taken to upon being liberated from the "Death Train".

I told her, "I do remember waking up early in the morning, to the lovely sound of church bells and the crowing of roosters greeting the rising sun."

She turned to me eagerly and said, "I believe I know the place. It is a hotel now. A new building was added to an older two story pre-war structure. It is just a few minutes away." We drove on, passing by an old, charming church; she stopped in front of it and remarked, "I believe this is the church whose bell you must have heard."

Francoise and Stephen at Seeshaupt Memorial.

Soon we arrived at the hotel, where she parked and we stared at the building. I strained my memory trying to remember. In front of us stood the hotel entrance, and to my right was the new building, attached to the old two-story structure on the left. It had been 50 years ago, when I was taken here unconscious; I could have not seen the outside. But as I looked to the second story, I noticed a bulge of three windows jutting out of the building. A shiver ran through me, and I thought that maybe I was trying too hard to remember. Registration was to the right as we entered the hotel, and a staircase led upstairs into the old parts of the hotel. My host and Françoise kept the proprietor busy and they walked into her office. I was alone. I took a few steps left, leading into the old part of the building and had almost reached the second floor, when I suddenly felt my chest tightening up. I was almost trembling as I opened the door to a room facing the street. My emotions overcame me as I remembered the alcove and the three windows overlooking the street. All of a sudden, I was back in 1945, on April 30th. From my daze, the sound of a church bell woke me up. "My God! 50 years ago I almost died here!" I thought.

We left the hotel and Françoise remarked as we entered the car, "You look like a ghost!

What happened to you?"

"I might have seen one," I replied, and explained the experience I had just gone through. It was an emotional trip that I will remember for the rest of my life. Every time we return from Germany I come back with memories that have been re-opened by unexpected circumstances. I'm lucky to be able to turn these experiences into positive thoughts. As soon as we got back to Las Vegas we resumed our normal life. We had enough time to relax, and prepare for the arrival of relatives from Canada.

Visit from Canada and Sad News from Hungary

In 1995, Françoise's sister, Liliane and her husband, Roger visited us from St. Hillarie. We showed them around, and enjoyed seeing them enjoying what Las Vegas has to offer.

Unfortunately, Liliane got affected by the air-conditioning, and developed pneumonia. She DID fully recover before they returned home.

In 1996 I got sad news from Hungary that my Uncle Charles had passed away. I started to prepare the diary and writings I had kept secret from my Uncle Charles ever since my liberation. My daughter Michele tried her best to help me with the grammar, correcting some of my writing.

In 1997, Daryl and his family moved to Las Vegas, where they bought a home not too far from us.

Fifteen

I got a telephone call from Pahrump, Nevada; a teacher from a local middle school invited me to speak in front of the student body about the Holocaust. I remembered the promise that I had made to my dying brother Andris, when he said, *"Share your diary with the world, and let them know the importance of family value and freedom."*

I felt the time had come to keep that promise, so I accepted the invitation with Françoise accompanying me. It was a sixty mile drive to Pahrump. I had "butterflies in my stomach" and so many questions; Will I know what to say? Will they understand my accent? Would I have the right answers to their questions?

When we arrived, the English teacher led us into a classroom with about 40 students in attendance, who all greeted us. Then I was on my own facing the audience. I thought of Andris and his smiling face. I knew nothing would stop me from keeping my promise to him. I felt better as soon as I introduced myself, "I'm Stephen Nasser, a Holocaust Survivor." That statement opened a hidden door into my memory and I started to re-live my past. I could not believe it when an hour had slipped by. The teacher signaled me that I had about five minutes left. I didn't even have time to take a deep breath before I was rushed by boys and girls, getting many hugs and thanks for sharing my life experiences with them. Some of them were still sniffing and wiping their tears.

I had a feeling that this speaking engagement was just the beginning of many to come. I got all the related papers together from my former diary and followed the necessary steps to have it published. I didn't have to keep the diary's contents a secret any more, since my uncle had passed away.

I started to get more invitations for speaking engagements from other schools, some from Pahrump, and some from Las Vegas. The word started to spread. Month after month, I got more experienced as a speaker, and had no doubt that my words had a positive effect on my audiences. I continued my efforts more than ever to have my book published. At my lectures, I mentioned my diary, which had now become my book, and many people put their names on a waiting list to be notified when the book would be published.

My first draft was 330 pages long. I located a retired English teacher to review it and make some corrections. She wanted to help me and kept her charges very reasonable. I had several copies printed and I mailed them out to publishers and universities. All the replies from the publishers were the same, "We do not accept unsolicited materials". I finally hired an agent in Los Angeles. We signed a year's contract, on a percentage basis; unfortunately, he promised a lot and did NOTHING. At the end of the year I terminated the contract. In the following years I sent out 81 copies, mainly to university libraries. It was somewhat discouraging to read all the "Thank you, but no funds available" replies.

Françoise and I kept busy fulfilling speaking engagements. I'd read a couple of newspaper articles about my lectures, and I didn't give up, despite the difficulty of getting the book published.

Israel, Egypt, Petra, 1998

I thought that in the future, as the lecture requests increased, and after the book would be published, our free time would be reduced, so we decided to take a long vacation and travel while we could. In Las Vegas we met an Egyptian travel agent, and he put together an attractive itinerary for us.

First we flew to Budapest, Hungary, and stayed for three days. From there we planned on visiting, Cairo, Egypt, Petra in Jordan, and spending a week in Israel. Our flight to Cairo started out great, but I thought we should be landing sooner than we were. I asked the steward why it was taking so long. He explained that there was a violent sandstorm in Cairo and its vicinity, and we were deferred to land in Cyprus.

Once we landed in Cyprus, the Hungarian crew handed us over to the Egyptians, so we could continue on an Egyptian aircraft when it became available. They checked us into a nice hotel, and we got settled into a comfortable room. After lunch, most of us wanted to take the opportunity to explore Cyprus. The authorities warned us, that if we left the hotel, and the Egyptian plane arrived to pick us up, we could miss the flight. Our flight finally took off past 10:00 P.M., and arrived in Cairo after 2:00 A.M. The brother of our travel agent was supposed to pick us up, on the previous morning, but of course the delay upset the plans.

Checking through emigration, the officer examining my passport was delighted to see my "Nasser" name. (Their president's name was Gamel Abdul Nasser.) He made a comment, "With that name you could not be Hungarian."

I sharply remarked, "That is the country of my birth; we were the only Nassers in Hungary. If you think that is unusual, on top of it I'm Jewish!"

He gulped, quickly stamped my passport, and looked the other way, calling out to people waiting behind me, "Next!"

Sizing up our situation, being in a strange, not too friendly nation, I got to a telephone, and with the help of an English speaking person, I called the contact number of the brother of our agent. I must have awakened him, by the sound of his voice. He was glad to know we were safe in the airport. He warned me, "Stay put where you are. Outside is not a safe place to be."

By 3:30 A.M., we were checked into a comfortable hotel. The following day when he picked us up for lunch, he apologized, and explained. "I called the airport and I was told that you were flown to Cyprus, because of the storm. They had no idea what day or time you would arrive in Cairo. It didn't matter what time you called me, as I was pleased to know that you two landed safely."

The following day we visited Giza, and the Egyptian museum, and also we both rode a camel.

We were exhausted by the time we got back to our hotel. The following day we took a flight to Abu Simbel, where in front of our eyes spread the old Temple of Ramses II. The Egyptian government, with international help, saved the complex of the Twin Temples and moved it to its new site 200 meters further, and 60 meters

Francoise and Stephen in Giza, Egypt.

higher, to allow Lake Nasser to be created, averting the flooding and possible destruction of the 3,200 years-old treasure. It was an unbelievable accomplishment! The engineers built an artificial mountain on top of it. We visited Lake Nasser, and afterwards, took a seven day Nile cruise. The number of tourists was way down, because of the massacre that killed 60 tourists in 2007 at the Temple of Queen Hatshepsut. About 80% of the cruise ships were idle. We had a very impressive tour of the Nile Valley, including Luxor, and the Valley of the Kings.

After our cruise, we crossed into Jordan, and stayed in Amman overnight. The following morning we arrived at Petra. We had a choice of riding the last mile to the entrance of the high cliffs either by cart, camel or horseback. Françoise and I enjoyed the horseback ride, and then dismounted and continued on foot. The high cliffs dwarfed us in deep shade as we curved through the pass. At the towering end, as the cliffs opened, an unbelievable sight came into view, the "Library", a multi-storied, pillared structure carved into the red rocks of the opposite mountain side, surrounded by the ancient ruins of the city, Petra. It took us a full day to see the sights.

We continued our trip through the Allenby Bridge and crossed into Israel. Finally, I felt safe, even though we were surrounded by neighboring countries, sworn to destroy the State of Israel. But like I say at my lectures, **NEVER AGAIN**. Fifty-three years ago the Holocaust ended, with six million Jews and five million other human beings massacred by the Nazi Bullies. Today modern Israel stands, with a mighty and dedicated Air Force, Army and Navy, which have been challenged several times. It is a miracle that despite being outnumbered by millions of neighbors, they stand firm holding the only Democracy in the Middle East. Sometimes they are denounced worldwide, "How dare they defend themselves causing harm to their invaders?" I felt proud to walk within their cities. We visited the Golan Heights, and Masada, and modern Tel Aviv. In Jerusalem we spent a whole morning at Yad Vashem, the greatest Memorial Museum dedicated to remembering the Holocaust.

Francoise and Stephen at Yad Washem Israel.

I located my family members in the Archive, which was a solemn experience. In the afternoon we marveled at the beauty of Jerusalem. Most buildings were hewn out of the typical white rock, which gives a glistening impression to the city. The following day we floated in the Dead Sea and visited the Masada. We needed a full day to see Bethlehem with its holy sites, Christian, Moslem and Jewish places of worship. The Israelis make it accessible to all human kind. We also spent a night in a Kibbutz, where hey had a motel available to visitors that was very up-to-date. My Cousin George's son, Andrew, lives there with his family, and works for Al El Airlines. We had a lovely family dinner and the conversation flowed into the evening. Our exciting vacation came to an end. We were much enriched with memories, as we returned back home to Las Vegas.

In October, 1999, our first great-grandchild, Kenneth, was born to Andrea. In December 2002, Andrea had a baby girl named Mikayla. Our family was growing

Publishing the Book 2002-2003

I met with an English professor who went through my manuscript entitled, **My Brother's Voice**, and now I had the final revision before publishing. In 2002 I got an email from Reno, Nevada and the librarian who had received my manuscript invited me to speak at the University. I accepted, and they flew me to Reno in the morning, to return the same day. It was a great success, and I got many more names on the book's waiting list.

The librarian gave me a suggestion, "I've read your script, and it is a great story.

Unfortunately, we have no funds to spend to publish your book here in the University.

However I heard that in Las Vegas, the major newspaper, *The Review Journal,* just opened a book publishing division, Stephen Press. Give it a try and let me know how you manage."

I thanked him for his suggestion and I made an appointment with the president of Stephen Press, Carolyn Huber. She received me in her office where I answered lots of her questions. Then she said, "Leave me your manuscript, and after I read it I will give you a call."

During the next few days Françoise and I anxiously awaited her call, although in the meantime, I had some more speaking engagements, by now totaling over 60 lectures. Finally Carolyn called me and I met her in her office.

I sat down across from her desk, just holding my breath as she said, "We are only publishing Western-related books." She paused and looked at me. Then she went on, "However, I'm making an exception, because your book has got to be published, it is a gift to society." She stood up and offered her hand. I nervously shook hands with her. Then she continued, "So sorry, about what happened to you and millions of others. Congratulations on your achievements. We will send you a contract to be signed by you and your associate, witnessed by a Notary."

Françoise and I celebrated the long awaited occasion. We toasted with a glass of champagne, and as I lifted my glass to the sky, I felt the presence of Andris, my brother.

A month later, Carolyn drove up to our house and delivered a box of freshly printed copies of **My Brother's Voice**. It was hard to believe that after keeping the diary a secret for fifty years; finally I had fulfilled my promise to my brother, "Share it with the public". I had a list of people waiting to read the book. Large, half-page articles with the book's picture appeared in *The Review Journal.*

Meanwhile, I had to fulfill many speaking invitations. I had made commitments to several schools in San Jose, California. I was 72 years old and my personal physician kept an eye on me, requiring annual checkups. A few days before leaving on our trip to San Jose, I got a call from my primary physician Dr. Garry Grossman. He advised me to take an angiogram, to rule out some suspicions as a result of my latest stress test. I acknowledged his request but delayed my examination.

Françoise and I drove to San Jose and stayed there for four nights with my cousin Carol and Mike. Mike arranged several lectures and accompanied us to most of them. Carol made us welcome in their lovely home and spoiled us with her good cooking. On Friday night she made a Sabbath dinner. We were able to meet their son, Joe and his family. After finishing our speaking engagements with about 2,000 students in attendance, Françoise and I drove back to Las Vegas, to face any medical problems I had.

On my return, I went to Valley Hospital in December, 2003, and had my angiogram. The result was positive; I needed heart bypass surgery. My family was summoned, as according to the diagnosis, I needed a quadruple bypass. During the operation, doctors harvested an artery from my left leg and used it for the bypass. After I was wheeled out of the recovery room, I saw my family waiting to see me. I had a smile on my face even though I could not talk, so I put my thumb up to say hello. I was informed that the surgeons actually had to perform a quintuple bypass. Dr. Grossman informed me that even though I had never had a heart attack, I could have suffered one at any time, during one of my lectures in front of students. I figured my best Friend up there, and Dr. Grossman saved my life, to complete my mission that I had promised my brother.

Françoise stayed with me daily from morning till night, while I was in the hospital. She just drove home to sleep. On the third day I took a walk in the hallway with Françoise's assistance. We returned to the room and I got into bed. I still had a tube inserted just under my rib cage. A doctor came in to remove that tube so I could be discharged the following day. She told me that it was just a routine procedure. She removed the tube and applied a pressure dressing on the opening, and secured it with a wide gauze bandage around my waist. She assured me that the wound would heal in a couple of days and the bleeding was stopped by the pressure treatment. I was served dinner sitting in a chair. Françoise was sitting facing me, and we were talking about my departure on the following day.

The nurse who picked up my tray called out in an urgent voice, "Your dressing is full of blood!"

The head nurse returned quickly and removed the dressing soaked with blood. She examined my open wound and could not explain why the blood would not clot. With the help of other nurses, the wound got re-wrapped. I got back in the bed and lay quietly on my back. In about fifteen minutes or so, I felt pulsating around the wound but no pain. Then I had a feeling as though it had started to bleed again. I had a nurse beside me monitoring my blood pressure so I calmly informed her about the pulsating feeling. Françoise, being a nurse, demanded that the doctor be notified of my condition. He was finally reached by telephone and gave instructions. By now I had a couple of attending nurses trying to stop the bleeding as they followed the doctor's orders. It was getting to a critical stage where a blood transfusion was considered.

I was feeling very calm, but I was worrying about Françoise. I asked her to go home and rest. "I will be fine," I said.

She was very firm. "Stop talking! I will spend the night with you here."

Knowing her, I knew she would not leave me, so I just squeezed her hand. It was almost 1:00 A.M. The bleeding had not stopped, just slowed down. The nurse called the doctor again. He ordered that all dressings be removed from the wound. They had to use a "Dutch Boy" method; two nurses alternating every fifteen minutes had to place a sterilized gauze-covered finger in the wound.

I was getting very weak and sleepy. In my mind Andris appeared again saying, *"Not yet, Pista."*

I opened my eyes, and saw Françoise watching over me, gently holding my hand.

In reassuring voice, she said, "While you slept, the nurses stopped your bleeding, you are out of danger. Just close your eyes and go back to sleep and I will sleep here beside your bed. I have a comfortable reclining couch."

My Speedy Recovery

By some miracle, I was home two days later. From then on I recovered rapidly. My wound healed, but not as quickly as I wished it would. I was walking around, taking showers and slowly returning to my normal life. I just knew my good Friend above did not want me yet. I had my life's mission to follow, and to keep my promise to my brother.

The holidays came and passed. It was 2004, and our calendar was crowded with speaking engagements. I started to receive out of town invitations from California, Arizona, and Utah.

I spoke about Family Values, Appreciation of Freedom and how I was able to write my Diary under the nose of the Nazis. I put together a power-point presentation containing some family photos, historical pictures of the Concentration Camp and my liberation picture I'd received in 1995 on our German trip. *The Las Vegas Review Journal* published pictures and articles about the book and my biography.

Book Promotion Across the U.S. and Canada

Françoise and I decided to drive to Canada and to promote my book across the United States. I consulted my cardiologist, and he declared me fit for the long drive. We locked up the house, leaving our car in the garage, and packed a few boxes of *My Brother's Voice* in the motor home's extended trailer and then we were fully prepared for our long journey. As we decided to make it a pleasurable trip with stops at many attractions and sights on the way, we took Route 66, the old historical highway. The Grand Canyon was a memorable stop, as Françoise and I are both fascinated by caverns of all types. At Seligman we took Highway 40, running from coast to coast. We belonged to a camping club, so we stopped by convenient places daily where we hooked up the motor home to water, electricity, and sewer. It had become a routine task, since we'd bought the vehicle in 1993.

We stopped in Flagstaff, Arizona at Woody's Campground, and then drove to the library, where I introduced myself to the head librarian as an author and a Holocaust survivor. In a few minutes, I'd created enough interest that the librarian requested a copy of my book. Altogether, I've approached over 70 libraries nationwide, and each has requested a copy. Every time I've faced a librarian, it was a challenge to determine the correct approach and to convince them to order a book. I had 'butterflies' in my stomach, but after a while, it became routine. I am convinced that I'm doing the right thing for the readers, and for future generations. Françoise encouraged me a lot; she was always there to support me. In my private moments, I felt Andris was proud of me. That feeling gives me insurmountable energy.

In Arizona, we marveled at the Painted Desert and the Petrified Forest, taking lots of video and still pictures. The scenery was breathtaking! Driving became an adventure, not a chore. We enjoyed cooking in our home on wheels, putting a roast in the oven, and in an hour or two, pulling over to eat as the aroma of the cooking meat made us hungry. We were care-free, and thought life was beautiful!

Since our motor home was only 21' long, we had no problem parking, so we spent a couple of days in enchanting Albuquerque, New Mexico. We enjoyed looking and shopping for souvenirs in the local art stores and mixing with people. Our next stop was in Amarillo, Texas and then we continued on to Oklahoma City. It became a habit to cook breakfast and then enjoy looking through the window as we ate, sitting at our cozy, upholstered booth. It took about half an hour to disconnect our 'home', and usually by 10:00 a.m. we were ready to roll, looking for new adventures ahead. In Arkansas, we made a side trip to the Hot Springs, where we unwound and both had rejuvenating treatments at one of the spas. By now we had driven about 1,500 miles, so we stopped in Little Rock and "stretched our legs" before we continued. After crossing into Tennessee, we made a short stop in Memphis and camped overnight in Nashville, also spending time at the "Country Music Hall of Fame".

After passing through Knoxville, we took Highway 81 toward Washington, D.C. We were in luck and found a campground near the highway. The subway was walking distance from the camp ground, and it took us just over half an hour to get to the National Mall with its reflecting pool. Here were lots of magnificent sights to see, the Capitol, the While House, and the Lincoln Memorial. Walking through the Holocaust Museum, I did not need a tour guide as I explained the exhibits to Françoise. At times it was very emotional and with my loving wife by my side, I felt the nearness of my family, watching from above. Next, we visited the Smithsonian Museum, which is a 'must see' for everyone. Then, we headed to Baltimore, where we pulled into an apartment complex, and rang the doorbell of my cousin Daisy's daughter, Klara.

After introductions, Klara and I had a lot to talk about. We met her son, Laser and daughter, Judy. It was heartwarming to be in the company of some remaining family members. Klara showed us around the next couple of days, as we visited the Harbor and enjoyed the city sights.

After our good-byes, we headed for New Hampshire, and spent a few days with our good friends, Adriane and Joe. They have a lovely home on 60 acers. We have visited them several times, by ourselves and with

Françoise's parents. On one of our previous trips, she had sent a present to my daughter Michele, a pedigreed pure white, Siamese kitten. My daughter adored that precious kitten and named her "Buttons". After spending some family time with Adriane, and Joe, we continued driving to Canada. Our first stop was Quebec City.

Françoise has two sisters; Lilane lives in Mt. St. Hillarie near Montreal, Monique in Quebec City. She and her husband Blaise live in a cozy, nice, single-story brick house, in the suburb, overlooking a well-kept garden. We spent several days in their home, and were spoiled by their hospitality.

Blaise drove all four of us to the Château Frontenac built in 1893. It dominates Quebec's skyline, overlooking the St. Lawrence River. There is a large square in front of the hotel, where local artists exhibit and sell their paintings. Below the hotel we took the Funicular, and exited into a store. The street outside was a tourist paradise, lined by boutiques and many varieties of unique shops. Street musicians and eateries created a charming setting. We drove to Sainte-Anne-Beaupre Cathedral, which was build around 1670. It has been credited by the Catholic Church with several miracles, so at the entrance there are many abandoned wheelchairs and crutches.

Monique and Blaise are gourmet cooks, and we gained a few pounds to prove it. From their house it was a comfortable drive to Liliane's house in Mount Saint Hillarie, noted for growing delicious apples. As we rang the doorbell, Liliane greeted us. We had a nice late luncheon sitting outside in her garden, overlooking mature trees, flower gardens and lilac bushes. We felt like we were at home. During a long conversation, Liliane remarked to Françoise, "Remember while Dad was still alive and with Mum, had their cozy two bedroom apartment? You two have stayed there on a couple of occasions."

Françoise let out a deep sigh. "Yes, those were the good old days. Unfortunately we cannot turn the clock backwards. Hasn't it already been two years since Roger passed away?"

Lililan nodded, "That is true. I'll be living alone until Marie Claude and her family will move in, after the addition to my house is completed in 2005."

Françoise knew a lot of nurses in the area that she had known for years, as they had all graduated at the same time. I drove her to Montreal and dropped her off at her 'Nurses' Reunion'.

All good things do come to an end, and we prepared for our long drive back home to Las Vegas, over 3,000 miles. On the way back we took a different route, stopping at more libraries and leaving books behind. We stopped at Sudbury, Sault St. Marie, Ontario, Cudahy, Minnesota, and Chicago, Illinois. There we were re-united with a relative, Ruth Nassau. Before the war she was our family's guest in Budapest. We had to move on, as we still had a long way to go. We stopped in Aurora, Denver, Grand Junction, Cedar City, and St. George, Utah. All together, we drove 8,815 miles.

Sixteen

I received a telephone call from California from Stephen Spielberg's office. They were calling in reference to the fact that I was listed in their records as a Holocaust survivor and had been interviewed and taped a few years back by the Shoa Foundation. The caller was encouraging me to speak at schools to help the cause the Foundations stands for. I informed her that I had spoken on dozens of occasions and was still doing so. She wanted to know if I had any speaking engagements coming up in the near future. I informed her I had a lecture taking place in the Flamingo Library in Las Vegas just a few days away. She was interested and asked me if it was all right for her to fly down to listen to me. I told her it would be my privilege to have her, just mention at the door that she is my invited guest.

The day of the lecture, Françoise and I arrived half an hour ahead of time. To our surprise, I had a dressing room assigned to me with my name on the door. Inside was a large bouquet of flowers, but I'm not used to such a fancy reception. It didn't take long before I got the five minute warning notice to get ready. I entered the stage area, and there was a fair-sized crowd waiting for me. I got through the lecture in an hour, followed by a question and answer period and book signing. The representative from

Spielberg's office applauded me for the important work that I'm doing. She was amazed that no organization was supporting me and that I did this all on my own, with the help of Françoise, my wife.

I signed a complimentary book for Stephen Spielberg. She took the book with her and said, "I will make sure he gets it, but I have to tell you, he has hundreds of manuscripts unread in his office."

We spent the summer at home and went to our favorite timeshare in Laguna Beach, California. Since we bought it in 1984, we have not missed spending time during the summer there. We stay once a year for a full week and enjoy our balcony overlooking the blue Pacific. Laguna annually has an Artist Festival called "The Pageant of The Masters." We have never missed it to this day.

Hispanic Congregation & Mexicali

I got a phone call from a gentleman who had met me on a previous occasion. He wanted to know if I would be willing to speak to his Hispanic-Christian church in Las Vegas and brought it to my attention that most of the congregation did not speak English well. He would have an interpreter to translate from English to Spanish. To me it was just another challenge, so I accepted. Françoise and I attended and arrived, as always, half an hour early. I had to allow for an accurate translation so I spoke very slowly and only a couple of sentences at a time. I considered the difficult job of the interpreter. I was standing in front of the congregation much longer than I was used to. It looked like the audience re-lived my experiences and became part of my message. I saw some boxes of Kleenex being passed around. The emotions of the people were obvious. I can't remember when so many people of an adult audience lined up, hugging me, and giving me warm handshakes.

After the lecture we were invited to participate in their buffet reception. We ate at the table with many strangers and our host and his family. They insisted on serving us, because we were the honored guests. They made us feel like a part of their family.

The Pastor of the congregation called me a few months later and invited me to speak in Mexico, near Mexicali. He explained that the people down there had hardly ever heard of the Holocaust. He thought I would be the perfect individual to share my story with them. He was going to pick us up from our house in his van and drive us all the way to Mexicali. I would speak in their sister congregation and we would stay in a local hotel for two nights. We agreed.

It was a very long drive there and back. I offered to drive part of the way to give the Pastor a break. After a good night's rest he drove us to the local congregation. To our surprise, the podium was well decorated. Beside the flag of Mexico they also had on display the blue and white Israeli flag. To top it off, there was a large Star of David in front of the podium.

We were supposed to start at 2:00 P.M., but at 2:30, we had less than fifteen people in the audience. My host Pastor could not understand the poor showing and he told me that he was waiting for two buses, coming from as far as Tijuana. Around 2:45 the buses arrived. They had had some engine problems. Suddenly, the hall filled up. I had an interpreter, and repeated my previously used speaking technique. My reception was very warm. These people also had very little knowledge of the Holocaust. It made me feel good to keep my promise to my brother, Andris, and to help many people to appreciate their families and freedom.

Exiting News from Stephen Spielberg Foundation

It was an ordinary Monday morning, and we were sitting at the kitchen table having our breakfast, reading *The Las Vegas Review Journal*, sipping our freshly brewed coffee. The phone rang and Françoise answered it. She excitedly covered up the receiver and whispered to me, "It is from the Stephen Spielberg Foundation."

I took the phone and a pleasant feminine voice was audible. "Mr. Stephen Nasser?"

I replied with a positive answer, "Speaking."

She continued, "Our office received an inquiry from Sydney, Australia. Somebody who read your book wants to get in touch with you. He claims to be your childhood friend. We informed him that all information about you is personal. He gave us his email address and telephone number. His name is Jancsi Markus."

I was overwhelmed. The lady asked me, "Are you O.K.?"

After a few seconds when I had recovered, I assured her, "I'm fine, it is hard to believe that after 40 some odd years, I hear from my best childhood friend. His father, Dr. Tibor Markus was my pediatrician."

She continued "It is our pleasure, to be of any help. By the way, I'm the one who listened to your lecture in the Flamingo Library, not too long ago. As I promised you, I gave your signed book, *My Brother's Voice* to Mr. Spielberg, who is a very busy man."

I could hardly wait to call Jancsi. Sydney is 18 hours ahead of Las Vegas time. I made my call anxiously waiting to see if someone would answer. "Markus residence, Johnny speaking."

I swallowed hard and exclaimed in Hungarian, "Jancsikam, it is Pista, Pista Nasser from Las Vegas!"

I heard a short pause. "Pistukam I can't believe we found each other!" We talked about our childhood, and Camp Muhldorf, where we met for a couple of days during our imprisonment, switching back and forth from Hungarian to English.

Australian Reunion

Françoise and I planned a long Australian vacation, as this was our chance to discover Australia, and meet my friend Jancsi (Johnny.) We made our preparations, booked our itinerary through a travel agency, and arrived at a hotel in Sydney. During our travel to Sydney, our tour guide showed a lot of interest in our upcoming meeting with Jancsi. After our arrival, she could hardly wait to give him a call. When she had him on the line, she handed me her telephone.

Jancsi and I arranged a meeting at Bondi Beach, in front of the main building. Our tour guide explained to the other group members, that on the following morning she would be joining us on the bus ride to Bondi Beach.

The following morning, when we all had breakfast in the hotel's dining room, even some traveling companions wished us good luck with my historical meeting with Jancsi. On the bus I was telling Françoise and our guide, some stories from way back, when Jancsi and I were about four years old. He was a year older than I. I talked about his bushy brown hair, and warm personality.

When we arrived, our guide got off first and I helped Françoise off the bus. Françoise followed me, as I searched for Jancsi, with the thick brown hair. Our guide was busy talking to this baldish, older person, about twenty feet away. She called out loudly, "Over here, I found Jancsi!"

I rushed over and hugged Jancsi tight as we didn't want to let each other go.

Finally Jancsi held me at arm's length, saying, "Pistukam I don't believe it, we meet again after all these years. What happened to your curly black hair? It is white as snow."

I replied jokingly, "At least I have hair, but look at you!"

Reuniting with Jancsi, Bondy Beach, Australia.

I could not finish my sentence, because Jancsi interrupted me. "But bald is beautiful!" He embraced Françoise, and suddenly we were kids again in our thoughts. We had a lot to catch up on, so we found a quiet corner in a nearby restaurant.

I told my tour guide, "We are skipping tomorrow's schedule, as we will go to Jancsi's girlfriend, Lily's house. The next couple of hours we spent together flew by.

l said a warm good-bye to Jancsi, and the three of us returned to the hotel. Our tour group stayed several days in Sydney, and we decided to spend that time with Jancsi and Lily. We had a lovely get-together dinner hosted at Lily's place, and spent our remaining time with them. They became our tour guides, and drove us to the modernistic Sydney Opera House. We marveled at the beautiful location of the Sydney Harbor, one of the nicest I've seen anywhere.

The Sydney Harbor Bridge is nicknamed the "Coat Hanger". It had tours scheduled by reservation only to climb to the top of the bridge, and Françoise and I were in luck as they had an opening in their busy schedule. We were secured with a belt attached to a cable, protecting us from plummeting to a watery grave way below. We climbed higher and higher on the cat walk, until we were on the very top. I do not like heights, but I took the challenge. Françoise was eager to climb the bridge. She loves all kinds of rides, even para-sailing. It was breath-taking, and I was glad we did it.

Francoise and Pista after walking on top of the Sydney Harbor Bridge.

We had lunch overlooking the Harbor and Jancsi introduced me to his daughter and family. During our never-ending conversation, he said, "By the way, you remember when we met at Muhldorf's

Concentration Camp, and I was in transit to the Wald Lager, and I had no place to sleep, and you offered me to stay in your narrow bunk bed?"

I looked at him and replied, "You know I've totally forgot, but you must be right, those days were brutal. We are lucky to be here and talk about it."

We had a great time with Jancsi and Lily, and invited them to stay with us in Las Vegas. The day to say good-bye arrived, and we left after hugging each other, with many pleasant memories.

Traveling the Vast Continent

The following day we went to Melbourne and Adelaide, and visited Kangaroo Island. We marveled at the huge eucalyptus trees, with dozens of Koala Bears hanging on the top branches like giant fruits. We continued our Australian coast-to-coast tour, by flying to the nearest airport to Ayres Rock, the huge monolith, also called Ularu by the native Aborigines. It was a short drive from our hotel to Ayres Rock. To enjoy the indescribable beauty of the change of colors, we arrived around sunrise with many others, and marveled as the monolith reacted to the rising sun. In front of our eyes we saw the mauve, change into purple and then to a golden hue. As the sun rose, it performed its magic, on Ularu.

Françoise exclaimed, "Nature is magnificent!" We did not climb the

Francoise and Stephen at Ayres Rock, Australia.

rock as many other tourists did. It is sacred to the natives.

Our journey continued as we arrived at the charming city of Perth on the West Coast, where we stayed several days at the home of our good friends, Diana and John, the couple we had met several years before on a European vacation. They spoiled us with their kindness. John drove us around the countryside, visiting local vineries nestled in between rolling green hills, and we stopped by some of his relatives and enjoyed their Australian hospitality. We had to say good-bye to our friends and they promised to visit us in Las Vegas (and eventually they did).

We flew back to the East coast to Cairn, and took an excursion to the Great Barrier Reef. It was an unforgettable place for underwater adventure. Françoise and I have snorkeled in many parts of the world, but the Reef topped them all. We enjoyed our health and youthful attitude, as I knew and felt that age was slowly catching up with us. I had a gut feeling that my brother was proud of us, to be able to travel, before we returned home to fulfill my promise to Andris and to keep speaking to the public repeatedly. This mission became our lifestyle.

Email from Australia, 2005

For many years during my question and answer period, I'm asked the date of my brother's death. I do not have the answer. He died in my arms before I was liberated on April 30, 1945. I tried, but could not put a date to when I lost him.

One morning as I was getting out of bed, Françoise called me from my office.

"Pista, you got an email from Jancsi in Australia."

I went into the office as Françoise handed me the printed version of the email. I read it out loud to share the information. "Dear Pista, I believe you have been looking for this information for a long time. My Cousin George found it while searching through the German archives on his computer. He found your brother's name- Andris Nasser. He died on March 30, 1945 from colitis." (The cause of death was fabricated, as there were no doctors. They just took the bodies and dumped them in mass graves.)

I paused and looked up to the sky and said, "Thank you, Andris for letting me know."

Then Françoise brought it to my attention. "He died on March 30, 1945. Do you know today's date?" she asked with amazement. "Today is March 30, 2005!"

We were both shocked- 60 years to the date. Was this a coincidence? Was it a message from Andris, or my best Friend above, who wanted me to know the date that I lost my beloved brother? The fact is I got this vital information in an email from Jancsi Markus, from

Sydney, Australia.

Sahara Library, 2006

I was invited to speak to guests of the Sahara Library in Las Vegas. There were about 80 chairs set up for the audience. When we arrived, there were a few chairs occupied. Steve Woolfston, a member of the Las Vegas City Council (today he is the Attorney General), introduced me. By the time Woolfston introduced me, the room was full with guests. I took the mike and started to speak. On the screen was the image of my book, *My Brother's Voice*.

When I get into my story I loose awareness of the audience, and I step into my memory. The years rewound to 1943, and I shared the events as I re-lived them in my mind. It amazes me how quickly time flies when I'm speaking, and before I know it; it is time for questions and answers. There were several hands raised, and I had no problem finding answers.

Mr. Woolfston, holding a large framed plaque in his hand, took the mike and spoke to me and to the listening audience, "On behalf of the City of Las Vegas, we want you to have this plaque, acknowledging your dedication to Humanity. We declare August 8, 2006 as Stephen Nasser Day in Las Vegas! Signed by the City Council and Mayor Oscar Goodman."

Blood rushed to my head, as I was overwhelmed. I called for help from the audience, "I don't feel right accepting such an honor; is there another survivor in the audience, who can share with me in accepting this plaque?"

One survivor stood up and came to the podium. He gave me moral support, as I received this symbol of gratitude. The whole audience rose, applauding. I do my lectures without any charge, but at times like this, I feel in my heart I have been compensated a thousand times over.

Fulton College

I got a telephone call from an agent explaining that Fulton College in Missouri would like me to schedule a speaking engagement there. They would pay all expenses and fly Françoise and me to their campus. We would have our own residence to stay in for three nights. I accepted and we flew to St Louis, Missouri. A car and driver were waiting for us at the airport and drove us to the campus in about two hours. We stopped in front of a stately residence, and our driver informed us that this was where we would stay for the next three days. He handed us an envelope with all of the instructions.

I notified my son who lived with his family in Missouri, within a few hours' driving distance that we were there. The following day Daryl's family arrived, just for the day, to listen to my scheduled speaking engagement.

The administration had advertised my lecture in the newspaper and on the radio. They expected about 300 people. We got to the spacious theater, and to my surprise, a few hundred people were already seated. After the introduction, I took the mike and started my hour-long presentation. The theater was packed with around 900 people. At the end of my presentation, I had a question and answer period, followed by the book signing. There was a long line at the table, and I was signing books for about three-quarters of an hour.

On the following day we were invited to the office. As we entered, a professor from Fulton College stood up and treated us very politely. He was in his late fifties, dressed in a dark suit with thinning gray hair. "Mr. and Mrs. Nasser? It is my honor to meet both of you, please sit down."

We made ourselves comfortable and I answered, "The privilege is mine just to be here, the alternative would have been disastrous. I'm just glad to be alive."

"Your lecture reached all of us; there weren't too many dry eyes. I know you have changed many lives for the better. The attendance was beyond our expectation."

I answered a few personal questions and we departed. I knew deep down that Andris must be proud of me. I'm keeping my promise.

Back Home Again

After we returned home we did not have too much time to rest, because the invitations to speak kept coming in. We visited many schools repeatedly, as the students changed, and advanced in age. After many years I became a household word, in several school districts.

We had family visiting from St. Hillarie, Canada. It was a pleasure to welcome the Ferron family, Marie Claude, Alain, and sons, Jean Philippe, and Vincent. They had planned their vacation in advance, and after arriving in Las Vegas, they rented a car, and toured the surrounding attractions. Finally we were able to welcome them in our house.

The following day we accompanied them on a hike in Red Rock Canyon. While we were hiking, Françoise lost her footing, and fell on her left arm. I insisted that our guests continue their outing, while I rushed Françoise to the hospital. She had a broken arm, after being treated temporarily, we returned home, where everyone was waiting anxiously for our arrival. On the following day, an orthopedic surgeon inserted two plates held by screws in her lower left arm. It was an unfortunate accident, but we all made the best of the circumstances. In a few days all of us left for Laguna Beach, where we had an enjoyable week; but, unfortunately Françoise had to stay out of the water. It was July 4th and all of us enjoyed the fireworks illuminating the sky. Our guests had a great vacation and returned home safely.

Speaking to the F.B.I.

One day I got a surprising request from an F.B.I. official, who asked that I speak to their local agents in the Las Vegas headquarters. Françoise and I had to arrive much earlier for security clearance and we assembled outside the main building. We did have a large audience, and at the end of my lecture, I got a standing ovation. On my power-point's last segment, on the screen, I have a large map of the U.S.A. in red, white, and blue, with the symbols of the armed forces. When that appears, I call on the audience to stand up and hold hands. Françoise and I join and hold hands with them. Then I say, "In the memory of over 470,000 U.S. soldiers who gave their lives for freedom, and all of our allies, and the 11,000,000 innocent civilians, who have been murdered by the Nazi bullies, please repeat after me, **NEVER AGAIN**." It was heartwarming to hear the roar of, *"Never Again"*, from these well-trained professionals. I received a signed framed certificate that I've added to my collection.

The pages of the calendar kept on turning, and strenuous hours of driving and speaking took its toll on us. We started to think about a vacation, this time for pleasure and relaxation. Françoise questioned me, "Pista, you're the one who is under lots of stress, making all the appointments and sharing your experience with the public. I know what your answer is, "I'm just keeping my promise to my brother." Don't you believe Andris, would like for you to take it easy and have a vacation and do other things instead of just speaking?"

I answered, "I never thought of it, but you put it in such a logical way, probably you are right. But let me tell you, I might be the one who speaks, but without your unselfish commitment, I would not be able to do it just by myself! You are right, let's have an unusual trip."

She continued, "Is there a special country in your dreams you would like to travel to?"

I thought for a while, and I remembered my dad. I shared my thoughts with Françoise.

"As little boys, Andris and I used to sit on the brown bear rug in front of dad's easy chair, with our ears wide open listening to his travel adventures. To us it was a special occasion. One day while he was talking to us, he stopped for a second and his eyes lit up, as he said, "After the war is over, I would like to take all of you on a photo Safari in Africa." He captured our curious imaginations. Andris and I could hardly wait to follow up on his remarks. We rushed to the bookshelves where he kept his Lexikons (encyclopedias). We sat at our desk and Andris eagerly looked up all the information on Africa, Safari, the Massai Tribe and the wild animals native to that area. We were so involved we did not realize dad was standing behind us, with a big smile on his face."

Françoise got excited, "African Safari it will be!"

Seventeen

African Trip

Soon it was time to plan a vacation, and we decided on a photo safari to Africa. Big Five, a travel agency, made all the necessary arrangements. We packed our bags and had the Sony video camera and the 8mm Olympus-still camera ready and loaded.

Our first stop was London, where we arrived early in the A.M. Our connecting flight did not leave till late afternoon, so we found an empty spot in a lounge to get some rest since we had flown all night. I made Françoise as comfortable as possible. While she was resting I kept an eye on our belongings, and bought a cup of coffee and sipped it slowly. After a couple of hours we reversed positions, and it was my turn to have a nap. By the time we got off the plane in Nairobi, Kenya, we were both totally exhausted.

We checked into our hotel, got into bed and slept till late the next morning. Finally we were well rested, but we almost missed lunch. There was a whole variety of strange food served buffet-style. Françoise is adventurous, so she had zebra for lunch. We noticed that high walls surrounded the large property of the hotel. Our guide, Tim warned us not to venture far if we left the hotel, and we took his advice. He was a native of Kenya, and a trusted driver and tour guide of the company. He briefed us on our itinerary for the next twelve days, and described the specially designed safari vehicle. The extendable roof had 360 degree vision, without glass, for unhindered photography. He also informed us that we had pre-booked reservations in various safari lodges with everything included.

After a couple of hours drive in the wilderness, we approached a Massai village, and saw some mud huts partly hidden behind a thick barrier of thorny thickets. Tim drove through the entry where the bushes were parted. We got out and met the tall, 6' plus, Massai Chief. Tim greeted him in his own language. The Chief spoke some English, and soon we were surrounded by young children clothed in garbs of native origin. I felt like we had stepped into a different time zone, a few centuries ago. We had brought Bic pens with us to give away to the children. Tim warned us earlier not to give the pens to the Chief, only hand them to the children, as otherwise the Chief would keep them, and the children would never see them.

The Chief spoke in broken English. "Welcome to Massai village…….. You give pens to Chief …………Chief will give to children." He reached toward the pens I had in my hand.

I pulled my hand back and told him, "I will hand one to each child."

Tim said something in the Chief's native language, and the children formed a line to receive the pens. After that, Tim led us into a native hut that had walls made out of crisscrossing sticks bound together with twine. The structure was covered with dried mud, and the roof was stacked with a thick layer of palm branches. We entered one of the huts and it took time for our eyes to adjust to the darkness. I saw only a narrow slit opening in the wall that served as a window. The bed was a stretched-out animal skin, attached to strong wooden sticks protruding from the dirt floor, elevating the skins about ten inches. Françoise and I looked around quickly and left, as the stifling air was too much to bear.

Outside we spotted a few warriors, with elongated ear lobes, leaning on their spears accompanied by some toothless elders, men and women. The group started to chant some rhythm, and swayed side to side. One elder lady extended her hand inviting me to be part of the dancing ritual. I will always remember her smile, exposing her gums with a few visible teeth. We took lots of pictures.

We drove on towards our safari lodge. Tim stopped several times so we could take pictures of giraffe, lots of zebras, and antelopes. We arrived at our lodge which consisted of several main buildings. We were back in the 20th Century!

Tim took us to our private, deluxe tent which was our home for a few nights. It was a very large permanent canvas tent mounted on a cement foundation. We entered a lower-leveled patio, furnished with wicker furniture and a table. Three steps up was our tent. To enter, we had to unzip two large flaps secured by a heavy-duty zipper. It was surprising to see that the tent had up-to-date furnishings: a dresser, a small table and two chairs, and a queen-sized bed. It had two large panel openings in the canvas that served as windows, covered by see-through netting, with rolled-up canvas on top for privacy. The rear end of the tent had a regular door leading into a fully equipped bathroom including a shower with hot and cold water. It was hard to believe that in the middle of the wilderness, surrounded by animals, we were sleeping in a tent and still had the comforts of home!

We had an early breakfast and Tim took us for our first game drive. We jumped to our feet when he pointed out our first lion and two cubs. He stopped and Françoise took some still pictures and I shot some videos, and then we continued. Tim was in touch with the other van drivers by walkie-talkie as they alerted one another when they spotted some unusual wildlife. Soon we stopped again and heard some crushing sounds, but saw nothing. Tim said, keeping his voice down, while pointing in the direction of the sound, "Have your cameras ready, there is a large bull elephant uprooting a tree."

The huge beast came into view, using his massive forehead and his trunk, as he appeared out of the brush.

The tree was tilted at an angle, its branches breaking and falling to the ground tearing the roots out of the soil. We watched and filmed with amazement until Tim drove off. We left quickly, before the elephant could decide to challenge our van. We had two

Charging Elephant South Africa

game drives a day, in the early morning when the animals are the most active, and mid-afternoon, when some of them were resting in the shade. That afternoon, we stopped by an adult giraffe and its young one while they were munching on leaves, pulling on the branches of a tree. We stayed in the van, taking pictures. None of us noticed that on the opposite side of the vehicle was a huge male lion. He used the rear corner of our van as a scratching post. Our van started to rock, while we held our breath. Luckily, the lion shortly disappeared into the bushes.

That night we had a reception and Massai show. These warriors jumped up to three feet while performing native war dances, to the beat of tom-toms. After a full day of activity, we fell asleep quickly; even the strange noises of the jungle night did not keep us awake.

The following morning, we rose very early and after breakfast, we took part in a hot-air balloon ride. At sunrise, six of us, standing in a large wicker basket, watched as the pilot fired up the flames with a roar, into the huge air cavity of our colorful balloon. The rise was gentle, and before we realized it, we were high above the landscape. The view was breathtaking. We did not need to gain any more altitude, and soon we were gliding over grazing fields that held zebras, antelopes, and giraffes. We watched as the balloon cast its shadow on the ground, moving gently, drifting with the air currents. Looking below, we saw that our balloon hovered over a herd of elephants. The animals must have sensed our presence as they kicked up a trail of dust and ran into a small, forested area. They must have felt safe in a meadow, as they stopped. We drifted over them again taking lots of pictures. Our pilot was in radio communication with a "chase vehicle." We landed in a flat meadow and climbed out of the basket as the vehicle arrived to pick us up. Our destination was a few miles away, where a scrumptious champagne brunch was waiting for us in the open field.

All six of us got into the vehicle, and the four-wheel drive moved cautiously in the uneven terrain. We drove over a small hill and started to descend. The vehicle got stuck on the slippery wet grass. We guys volunteered to push, so hopefully we'd be on our way again. As we opened the side door, we heard the screaming sound of hyenas. Our minds changed in a hurry, as we saw there were four of them, hungry for their next meal. It was amazing that each of the beasts stood a few feet from the corners of the vehicle, cornering us from four sides. The driver tried to rock the car by forwarding and reversing gears, but it did not help.

Then I got an idea and said, "We might have a chance if all of us stood up and braced ourselves holding onto the seats and handle bars. We should rock back and forth synchronizing with the driver." We got out on our second attempt, and left the scene in a hurry, leaving behind four hungry howling hyenas.

We continued driving on the uneven terrain, and in about twenty minutes we arrived in a valley with a few scattered trees. Chefs were visible in their traditional white hats. Our nostrils filled with the smell of our upcoming Champagne Brunch, in the middle of Africa. We were eager to get out of our safari vehicle, as we couldn't believe our eyes! In the middle of nowhere, we saw highly sophisticated cooking equipment, powered by a gasoline generator. There was a large tent-canopy that provided shade from the searing African sun. The tables were set with white linen, silverware, and glasses being filled with champagne. The smell of bacon and sausages and pancakes was incredible. The aroma of freshly brewed coffee filled the air. We had an unforgettable Champagne Balloon Adventure!

Our stay at the Lodge was outstanding. After an early rise and breakfast, we headed to the plush Kenya Safari Club, overlooking majestic Mount Kilimanjaro. A flat tire delayed us, but after a couple of hours of waiting, a truck stopped on that lonely dirt road and helped us out with some tools, which Tim was missing. Tim left us at the Safari Club, and we thanked him for his expert driving and guiding skills.

Our accommodations at the Kenya Safari Club were superb. We had our own bungalow with a living room and fireplace, a dining room, a large bedroom with a king-sized bed, and a spacious bathroom with a huge, built-in Jacuzzi tub. I had to wear a jacket and tie for dinner, and Françoise dressed in a nice cocktail dress. We were ready to walk to the elaborate dining area, when a servant in a white jacket rang the doorbell. He was sent to light our fireplace. Neither one of us was used to high style luxury like that, but we enjoyed every moment of our three-night stay.

The dining room was at ground level, and waiters in tuxedos, and white gloved attendants ushered us to our seats. There were eight of us seated at the elegantly set table. Soon after we were all comfortably settled, we introduced ourselves, sharing names, places we were from, and occupations. It was truly an international crowd. I stated my name and country and before I could finish my sentence, an American lady across from me interrupted, "Are you Mr. Nasser, a Holocaust survivor who wrote a book, *My Brother's Voice?*"

Françoise and I were shocked, and I was almost speechless. I answered, "Yes that is correct, my God what a small world!" From that point on, I was asked to answer more questions from curious people. We had a great dinner, fit for a king.

The rest of the trip, people stopped me several times, as they were curious about my Holocaust experience. The last leg of our adventure took us to Harara in Zimbabwe, where we stayed overnight in the hotel. The following day we were driven to Victoria Falls, where our accommodations were superb. From the hotel's terrace, we had a commanding view of the brush with scattered, intermittent meadows. Many types of wildlife were visible through our binoculars, and we could identify the different species. Further beyond, mist was visible, created by the vapors rising from the crushing cascades of Victoria Falls. We viewed the falls across from us, as the waters were rushing through the rocks, cascading down into the Zambezi River, creating a thunderous roar and leaving several spectacular rainbows.

Later, we took a helicopter ride, and the magnificent falls were dwarfed from high above. After our unforgettable stay at the falls, we returned to Harara where we bought a hand-decorated ostrich eggshell. In the airport, as we were checking through customs, Françoise was carefully removing the eggshell from a well packed plastic bag when the egg slipped out, hitting the tile floor. Even the customs officers looked shocked as the bottom of the egg shattered into many pieces. I was also devastated seeing our prized possession broken, only to be swept up and end up in the garbage. Instead, I picked up all the pieces, even though I was ridiculed by everyone. I took the pieces home, and today you can see the egg in my office. You would have to pick it up, and have a close look at it to see that the pieces are glued together.

Eighteen

Mingus High

I got an invitation from Mingus High School in Cottonwood, Arizona, so Françoise and I drove to the school. After checking in at the main office, we walked by the auditorium below us. Soon I would be on that stage, facing about 700 students, faculty, and some parents.

I set up my power point, and took my position on stage. The bell sounded and students, led by their teachers, were seated in an orderly fashion. All fell quiet and the principal introduced me. I had my remote and flipped the slides on my power point as I got into my presentation. As usual, time flew by. The audience had some questions, and I answered them all. I took my seat beside Françoise and the students lined up to purchase some books. After the book signing, we had no one else in line. But I noticed one student was hanging around, hesitantly, getting closer. I asked, "Can I help you young man?"

He lifted his chin and awkwardly asked, "Can I speak to you for a minute?"

I said, reassuringly, "Of course you can, come a little closer!"

He took a couple of short steps and I could see fear in his eyes. He started speaking, "Mr. Nasser, my name is Johann Becker, and I was born in Germany." He looked slightly downwards.

141

Without hesitation, I extended my hand and said, "Nice to meet you, Johann."

As we shook hands, I continued, "I'm Stephen Nasser and I was born in Budapest, Hungary. We all had to be born somewhere, you realize. Be proud of wherever you were born."

He looked up and replied, "But sir, your whole family was killed by the Germans."

I answered, "You are almost right as some Germans were involved, but it was mainly the Nazis."

He couldn't look me in my eyes and said, almost whispering, "Sir, but my Grandfather was a Nazi."

Then I questioned him, looking straight into his eyes, "Are you a Nazi?"

The reply came instantly, "No sir, but I have enough, living with this burden!"

I put both of my hands on his shoulders, and said in a strong, reassuring voice, "Young man, you have carried this burden long enough! You are not responsible for crimes created by others. As a Holocaust survivor, I want to lift the burden you have been living with. You are not responsible for the past. But the future is in your hands. Have a good attitude, and God Bless You."

He hugged me tightly and was shaking with tears as he let me go. He took a few steps and turned around with his thumbs up, forcing a smile to his face.

Health Food Store

I got a personal invitation from a local health food store. The owner mentioned that he expected only a handful of people, as they have a limited space for about 70. I accepted the invitation. I thought that even if I talked to a few people, they have friends and my message of family values and appreciation of freedom will be passed on. We set a date and time.

Just a day before the engagement, I got a call from the owner, saying, "Mr. Nasser, I just got a call representing the local Nazis, warning me that if I don't cancel, there will be at least fifty uniformed Nazis demonstrating in front of the store! What do you suggest we do?" she questioned.

I replied firmly, "If you are willing to go ahead as planned, I will be there. If they call again just tell them that Mr. Nasser said to bring all the uniformed friends they want.

As a matter of fact, bring everyone they know, the more the merrier. He is not afraid of "Paper Tigers."

That night the hall was filled to capacity. They ran out of chairs, so some people were left standing. Over thirty people had to be turned away. Even Carolyn Huber, my publisher, came to listen. I didn't find out until after the event that the store owner had notified the authorities and two F.B.I. agents were in the crowd. It was a great get-together, with the usual question and answer period, and book signing.

Molasky Middle School

Ann, an English teacher at Molasky Middle School, invited me again. We had met a few years back and became good friends. Françoise and I, and Ann and her husband, Leigh Raskin got along really well. She is devoted to her students' education. Whenever she needed me to speak about the Holocaust, I made myself available. We had about 40 students in the small auditorium, and she asked the students to be well behaved and respectful. I showed my power point presentation in about one hour. I felt very welcomed by the students and they asked intelligent questions. Ann invited me on numerous other occasions, and even to other schools where she taught during the summertime.

North Carolina

We received an invitation from a church in North Carolina (people who had listened to me during an ocean cruise, wanted to share their experience with their fellow congregation). Françoise and I flew there from Las Vegas. At the airport our host was waiting for us, and dropped us off at the hotel. The following day we were driven to the church's reception facility. As we entered the large room, we realized the congregation was well prepared. There were at least a dozen round tables with white tablecloths set up for a luncheon reception. We got seated at the head table decorated with fresh flowers, and after the introduction we had a delicious lunch.

Behind us was a small stage with a large projection screen. Soon after lunch, Françoise sat behind a table with my books and flyers. I took the microphone as the audience was anxiously waiting for me to start. After a question and answer period, and book signing, it took a while before we could get back to the hotel. The following morning we flew back to Las Vegas.

Budapest, Hungary River Cruise

We flew out of Las Vegas through Dallas, London, and Budapest, arriving at the Feri Hegy Airport. We took a taxi to our hotel which overlooked the Fisherman's Castle and the Royal Palace, built on a hill. From our room we had an excellent view of the Danube River, spanned by the majestic Chain Bridge.

The day of our arrival we visited my cousin Daisy. She had turned 92, but was still in good health despite her age. I'd witnessed her father's death, when a Nazi shot him dead in 1944, when we were interned at a brick factory in Buda Fok. Daisy's son, Tomas arranged a family get-together in a restaurant across the Danube River on the Buda side. I had another cousin, Andris who flew in from Sweden with his family, and a couple of other relatives. They had been lucky enough to be saved by Raoul Walenberg, a Swedish diplomat during the Holocaust, from being deported to concentration camps.

I was told about a memorial that was recently erected on the shore of the river. Françoise and I visited the site, near the bridge. We arrived and saw, on the concrete steps, rising from the Danube, dozens of shoes of all kinds: children's, ladies', and men's, molded in cast iron and secured to the top steps overlooking the Danube River. This monument represented the massacre of thousands of Jewish Hungarian citizens of all ages. The Hungarian Nazis, called Nyilas (Arrow Cross), lined up innocent civilians on the steps day after day, and they were shot and fell into the Danube River below. There is a large plaque written in English commemorating the murder of these souls.

We stayed on our ship for a couple of days and did lots of sightseeing. We took the subway to Ujpest, where I was born in Arpad St., 42. It used to be called "The Nasser House", and it is still standing.

Back on the ship we met some people who were familiar with my book. They must have notified the cruise director, because to my surprise she approached me and asked if I would speak to the passengers about my experiences during the Holocaust. She pointed out that many of the passengers were German, so it could be a very sensitive situation. She instructed the tour guides to ask the passengers, while they were returning on the bus from touring the city, if they were interested in listening to a Holocaust survivor, a fellow passenger, who would share his experience with them. The tour director left a sign-up sheet and pencil out in the boat's entry hall. Anyone wishing to attend my lecture could sign up. There were about a hundred and forty passengers on board.

Françoise and I were curious about the result, and around 4:00 P.M. we looked at the sign-up sheet and saw less than half a dozen names. About an hour later the tour director asked me if I could speak that evening after dinner. By that time, she had 138 fellow passengers signed up, so I agreed. After I finished my lecture, to my surprise, I got a standing ovation, and had to answer many questions. We only had one copy of the book with us, but afterwards we got twenty-eight requests to mail signed books, back to their homes, and everyone pre-paid me.

We mailed the signed books soon after we returned to Las Vegas. I mailed one book to a nice gentleman Jose Valdez in Guadalajara, Mexico. He made a point of meeting me after my presentation and asked me if I would ever consider lecturing in Guadalajara. He showed a special interest in reading my story.

Our riverboat tour took as all the way to the Black Sea and through the Balkans and Romania. We came home with a lot of memories, and I had many more invitations to fulfill.

Faiss High School

Faiss High School is a well-respected facility in Las Vegas. I have lectured there a few times in previous years. This time when Françoise and I entered the large gymnasium, the bleachers were already opened. We noticed that in front of the bleachers, there were about 80 chairs set up. Our teacher host greeted us, handed us a couple of bottles of iced water, and she remarked, "We have a surprise for you."

We sat behind our usual table. My host explained to us that the principal had ordered specially made shirts for the honor students. Soon, they started to enter. Some students wore black T- shirts with, **NEVER AGAIN** printed on the front, and "**11 MILLION**" on the back in bold white letters. They occupied the front row. Then she handed us a few of the shirts for us to wear. (Since then, we have worn these shirts for our lectures.) After the lecture we had another surprise. All the honor students wearing the black shirts formed a long line. The host teacher handed me a silver-colored marking pen. One by one I signed the back of each shirt. It was not an easy job.

We had a great lunch and mixed with the students who asked more questions. I got many thanks for all the advice I gave them for the future. We were very proud about how well the lecture went. I was sure that my brother Andris was the proudest.

Bishop Gorman

Bishop Gorman School is well known for its athletic and academic excellence.

Every second year, three speakers are invited for two days of lectures: a retired police detective, Randy Sutton, a theatrical producer,

Warren Lewis, and myself. Each day of the event I arrive at 7:30 A.M. in the morning. We do have a break for lunch and occasionally we visit each other's lectures. Most of the time I have a full auditorium of students, while the others speak to a selected group. The lectures are well advertised in the community and at each of my engagements parents are also invited.

Shadow Ridge High School

We were invited to Shadow Ridge High School, just a few miles north of our house. The host teacher introduced me to the students and I spoke for about an hour, and we had a question and answer period. As we were leaving the facilities, a young lady who was a teacher there approached us, "I know you are ready to leave, but would you consider speaking to my class of students? It would mean so much to me!?"

I thought for a minute, and obliged. The teacher, Tianna, thanked us for staying the extra time, and for speaking to her students.

Invitation to St. George

A few months passed, and I got a telephone call from the father of Tiana, Chuck Andrews in St. George, Utah. "Mr. Nasser, my daughter Tianna, could not stop talking about your lecture in Las Vegas, Nevada. Would you consider driving to St. George, and speaking to a community gathering? I would make the necessary arrangements. We would be honored if you would stay with us overnight."

I accepted. Susie and Chuck treated us with great respect. After staying overnight in their lovely English style home, Susie made us welcome with a delicious breakfast. We talked a lot, and got to know them and their extended family. Tiana was also there with her fiancée, Sam. That evening they drove us to our destination at a large mansion. The host and hostess were very friendly. Entering the spacious house, we were led into a huge room where dozens of chairs were set up to accommodate the invited guests. Chuck and Susie were sitting in front with Tiana and Sam. People kept arriving and all the seats were taken. After my lecture,

I had a lot of questions to answer. People lined up to buy copies of *My Brother's Voice*.

After we got back to our friend's house, before retiring, we all relaxed and had a friendly discussion. We were complimented because the lecture was a great success. In the conversation, Tiana and Sam's wedding was brought up. They invited us, and Françoise and I felt honored by the warmth the family radiated towards us. After my successful lecture in St. George, Utah, we fulfilled several other speaking engagements in Las Vegas.

Nineteen

TRAGEDY STRIKES AGAIN, 2008

It was October and fall was in the air. Françoise and I were looking forward to our long-planned trip to visit France and Normandy. I felt very strongly about paying my tributes to the fallen soldiers of World War II who gave their lives to defeat the Nazi Bullies.

First though, we had several engagements to fulfill in St. George, Utah in local and neighboring schools. We loaded our 2005 Prius with boxes of books and drove the 130 miles in two and a half hours. The highway took us through the Virgin River Gorge, which is nature's masterpiece, as the road crosses the river surrounded by steep, rocky cliffs on both sides of the road. We drove through Arizona and entered Utah, arriving at our friends' house, Susie and Chuck. They have been very kind to let us stay with them year after year.

The following morning we spoke at Dixie High School. We had about an hour and a half to rest and grab a bite to eat. The early afternoon took us to Desert Hill High, to a full assembly. I spoke about ninety minutes and answered lots of questions and signed many books. An enthusiastic audience, with boys and girls lined up, hugged me, and took pictures. I get this type of reception at most of my lectures.

The following day we drove to the small community of Hurricane where we have been invited annually to the high school and the middle school. The rest of the week we stayed in St. George, as we continued our speaking tour to Pine View Middle and Pine View High School, and Snow Canyon Middle School. Mill Creek High School was our last lecture before we returned to a well-deserved rest in our Las Vegas home.

A few weeks after the lectures, the class of teacher Bobby Mosteller, of Millcreek High, mailed me a replica of my lost diary. She had bought some used cement paper bags, and fashioned them into a very similar diary to the one that I had written at age 13 back in the camp. I was overwhelmed! Ever since, I use this replica of my original diary every time I speak.

My Diary recreated by Millcreek School, in Utah.

While I was driving home from St. George, Utah, Françoise was catching up by reading some letters from previous mailings. So far we have read over 11,000 letters from all over the U.S. and other international locations. We were about fifty miles from home, when she received a call on her cell phone from my daughter Michele. Françoise seemed very upset, so I tried to make out the nature of their conversation.

After the call my wife explained to me, "Michele wished us a good trip to Normandy next Wednesday. She said she wanted us to go, as she'd be all right, and we should not worry."

Françoise had asked her, "Why, what is wrong?"

Michele had replied, "I have a brain aneurism and my doctor is waiting for the results of the brain scan, before he will proceed with the operation."

Françoise exclaimed, "Oh my God, we were never told she had that condition! You are her father, what do you think?"

I replied quickly, "We are canceling the trip to Europe. I don't even want to stop at our house in Las Vegas. We are driving right through to California. It is 2:00 P.M. now; we should arrive around 7:00 P.M to see Michele in Chino Hills, California."

Françoise is a retired nurse and she agreed with me wholeheartedly. I stepped on the gas, and we left Utah and Nevada behind and drove to California. We got there at 7:00 P.M. and we were both very apprehensive as we approached the front door. Michele opened the door. She looked great so we breathed a deep sigh of relief.

Michele hugged both of us and said, "You didn't have to come, as I'll be fine. And I want you to take your trip as planned on Wednesday."

We asked her and her husband, Paul about her medical diagnosis. Françoise stepped closer to Michele and remarked, "Chele, it looks like your right eyelid is drooping."

She replied, "I'll go to the bathroom and check it out."

After a long wait, Paul went to investigate. "I'll be back in a minute," he said as he headed for the bathroom. A few seconds later, we heard Paul's distressed yell, "Call 911!!!!"

I jumped to the phone as Françoise ran into the bathroom to see what had happened. I heard a scream so I rushed into the bathroom and found Michele unconscious, lying on the floor with her eyes closed.

The paramedics took her to the closest hospital. After half an hour, they rushed her to Chino Valley Trauma Center. We waited anxiously, until her doctor called us into a private room and said in a solemn voice, "Michele is on life support, but she is gone. She was brain dead when the aneurism ruptured. There is nothing we can do."

His words stabbed me in the heart and I pleaded, "Doctor, please operate immediately." I looked up to the sky, to my best Friend, "Please don't let me lose my daughter!"

The doctor said almost in a whisper, "Mr. Nasser, Michele is brain dead and there is nothing anyone can do."

Françoise and Paul and I hopelessly embraced each other. The doctor said quietly, "You can go to her bed side. She is on life support. She still has a strong heart beat. If you watch the screen it will stay steady, but once it begins to slow down then it will descend quickly and when the line remains straight, that will be her final moment."

We located Chelsea, her daughter, who was working the Halloween Haunt at Knott's Berry Farm by calling park security who were able to find her. I talked to her and she was ready to jump in her car and drive about 40 miles to see her mother while she still had a heart beat. I was willing to drive to Knott's Berry Farm and pick her up. I said, "We don't need two tragedies in one night." She was 23 years old and very responsible, but time was running out, and she decided to start immediately for the hospital.

We then notified Michele's best friend, Mona. Paul, Françoise, and I were at my daughter's bedside, holding her limp hand and keeping an eye on the monitor when Chelsea arrived to see her mother alive for the last time. Shortly after, Mona, with her husband, Herb arrived. We helplessly watched the monitor slowing down and at 12:13 A.M. it flattened out. Paul lost his beloved wife; Chelsea, her mother; and I, my beloved daughter. I've been stricken by grief many times, but I was not prepared to lose my wonderful daughter. I just looked up to heaven and cried out, *"Andris please take care of my little girl until we all meet again."*

Reflecting back, it must have been God's will that we drove to Chino Hills nonstop, and had but seven minutes to hug Michele for the last time. I notified my son Daryl that his sister had passed away. The following day he flew to Ontario Airport, where we picked him up. Unfortunately he was not able to attend the funeral, because of medical reasons.

Thankfully, Françoise was by my side, giving me moral support. Michele was laid to rest at Hillside Memorial Park in Culver City, California. It was a sad, emotional ceremony. Her resting place is overlooking the graves of her beloved grandparents, Boobi and Zaida Cash. After the funeral we said an "aching" good-bye to our granddaughter,

Chelsea, and son-in-law, Paul, and my son, Daryl and drove back to Las Vegas.

The long drive flew by very quickly, as we conversed all the way home. Françoise was not Michele's biological mother, but they had had a very close relationship. She remarked to me, "We all lost a lovely person, but it must be very hard for a father."

I let out a deep sigh. "She was much more than a daughter, she believed in my mission, and put her soul into it, to help me keep my promise to Andris. As a high school student, she edited my diary, even though I kept it a secret from the public. After she got married and became a mom, she promoted me in the Chino area, in California, and secured countless speaking engagements for me in several schools."

Françoise replied, "She was very proud of you, and loved you very much."

I teared up and quickly turned off the freeway into a resting area. Françoise embraced me, as the onrushing memories kept haunting me. We rested a while, and Françoise insisted she drive the rest of the way. I regained my composure, and remembered Andris; he will take care of my "little girl". I still had to keep my promise, to force a smile onto my face, and make everyone proud up there, looking down at us, now including Michele.

After a few weeks, normal life resumed. I published a Teacher's Resource Guide and dedicated it, to "My beloved daughter, Michele Kim Nasser Jones". This guide became a tool in the hands of many teachers, to help them teach the Holocaust, accompanying my book, *My Brother's Voice*, which I had dedicated to "My Beloved brother, Andris".

Life had to go on, so Françoise and I decided to celebrate Michele's life by spending time with our family. I booked a cruise for Chelsea, Paul, Françoise and I, from San Diego to Hawaii and back during the Chanukah, Christmas, and New Year's holidays. We celebrated Michele's memory. She had always wanted to take this trip as a family; unfortunately, we cannot change history. In reality, there were only four of us on the cruise, but Michele was with us in our hearts.

We boarded Holland America's *Oosterdam*, in San Diego, California and spent several days sailing the blue Pacific. Father and daughter shared one cabin, and Françoise and I had a cabin close to theirs. We spent a lot of time together, but still we respected each other's privacy. While on shore, we enjoyed the tropical paradise. Chelsea had her camera focused on all the attractions the island had to offer, its lush green landscape, hidden waterfalls, the vast variety of birds and animals, including the smooth sandy beaches with the breaking surf, and some of the rocky cliffs, with their blow holes. We did not realize, but this trip launched Chelsea into a new career; today, she is a recognized photographer. I'm sure her mother is very proud of her!

We thoroughly enjoyed spending the holiday together as a family. This getaway gave Françoise and me a little break. On our return, we had many speaking engagements waiting for us in California, followed by Arizona, and Utah. In January, February, March, and April we are usually booked solid for many years. During this past speaking season, Françoise and I drove around 3,000 miles and held over 40 lectures. Additionally, we got invited to several local schools in Las Vegas. Even though most schools are closed for the summer, we do receive occasional invitations during that period. It was a trying year and Françoise and I decided to take a special trip in October.

Cruise to Antartica

A Norwegian cruise line had an excursion from Ushuaia to Antarctica, on a specially built ship capable of cruising to the frozen continent, anchoring near shore, and landing up to 300 passengers in Zodiac inflatable rubber rafts. We flew to Buenos Aires where we had a hotel room reserved for us. From there we took a short flight to Iguassu Falls, and saw the Argentinean and the Brazilian sides of these magnificent falls. We did see the thundering waters of Niagara, and we experienced the majestic flow of Victoria Falls in Africa. These falls stretch for miles, crossing borders. I described them like a mammoth layered cake as far as the eye could see, cascading from one level to another, with the final cascade ended up in a giant body of water creating a mist and glorious rainbows.

We got back to our hotel in Buenos Aires and the following day we flew to Ushuaia. There we boarded our small, but well-equipped cruise ship, *The Hortiguten*. Despite the fact that it was a smaller ship, the state-rooms and public rooms were luxurious! Every day we had a chance to listen to speakers who were experienced in the Arctic region. To our surprise we all got a gift, a waterproof, zippered jacket, with large white letters on the front displaying, ANTARTICA.

We made many friends, and the word spread quickly that I had written a diary during the Holocaust and it had been published as *My Brother's Voice*. Some people on the cruise came from Salt Lake City, Utah, and they requested that if I ever lectured in that area, to let them know because they would like to attend my lecture. I told them about my upcoming engagement near Park City, Utah.

We crossed Drake Channel, a dreaded area, well known for turbulent seas. It was rough, but we didn't complain. Before landing, we were briefed on strict international law. Only a maximum of 300 people were allowed on shore per day. After stepping on shore, no contact could be made with the animals, penguins, and sea lions, and we had to keep at least five feet distant from the animals. This was to protect the wildlife from viruses carried by human beings.

On the day of our landing, before boarding the Zodiacs, we were issued knee-high rubber boots. We had to walk through a long metal container filled with disinfectant. The liquid came up to about ankle height. The first landing detail returned from the shore about half a mile away in their motorized Zodiac. We got the final instructions that the crew had lowered a metal ladder into the water, just a couple of feet off the shore. It was not a sandy beach as there were lots of huge pebbles and rocks. As soon as the craft landed beside the ladder, one by one, each passenger held onto the crews' extended hands, stepped on the ladder and secured the first step into the frigid waters. Our knee high boots gave us ample protection.

To me it didn't sound too daunting. We were all very anxious to plant our feet on Antarctica, and we landed safely and all of us went on shore. It was like a dream with the snow covered landscape starting about fifty feet from shore. Dozens of curious penguins, not afraid of humans, waddled to meet us and satisfy their curiosity. We could not keep the required five feet distance from the "Tuxedo Clad" animals, as they came so close they were almost touching our boots.

We made seven landings at different areas and we visited a Polish base. Inside the metal hut, we observed some scientific equipment and living quarters. It was extremely educational. We landed at one spot where hot springs were bubbling up near the shore. The water was pretty warm in spots. Even though it was their Arctic summer, the air temperature was around 36F.

Back on board we had a relaxing dinner, and we had a lot to talk about with all of our experiences. The following day we cruised among beautiful blue-shaded ice floes, which were barely visible above the water line. Some massive icebergs were hundreds of feet tall, even larger than Manhattan Island. We learned that two-thirds of the icebergs are submerged, and only the top one-third is visible. Our ship looked like a giant besides the smaller, colorful floating ice.

Other massive icebergs dwarfed our ship, which then looked like a dinky toy drifting by. Some larger ice floes had hollowed arches and unusual formations highlighted by deep blue to lighter hues of a magnificent variety. Occasionally we noticed a few relaxed penguins and sea lions, as they lazily floated by. It was a nice calm, sunny day. Most of the passengers were leaning against the railing, with binoculars and cameras in hand, just enjoying an unforgettable day in Antarctica.

Than we heard an announcement, "This is the Captain. We are in luck as we are approaching a school of whales, so have your cameras ready. We have greatly reduced our speed and are just floating by."

All of us attentively searched the waters, and suddenly we spotted breeching whales, large ones and small ones. The icy waters were churning with white foam and bubbles, as the huge mammals surfaced and dove, one beside the other. We didn't have to look for the action, as it was all around us. I considered myself extremely fortunate as not too many people have the privilege of watching such a spectacle performed by nature. Françoise and I were speechless just looking on. How I wished Andris could have been beside me!

Twenty

INVITATION TO PARK CITY

I received another invitation, this time from Tiana; after their marriage they had settled near Park City, Utah. She was exited to inform us that her school district would like to invite us for a speaking engagement. They would cover all expenses if we would agree to fly to Salt Lake City, and we accepted the invitation. Sam and Tiana picked us up from the airport and drove us to our lodging; the winter scenery was breath-taking. The following day we successfully completed our lecture. Tiana also set up an engagement for a public audience in the local library in Park City. When we arrived, there were already people waiting. The attendants brought in extra chairs. Many guests had to stand if they wanted to stay. Just before the introduction, Françoise and I could not believe our eyes, as several people in the back row stood up, wearing jackets marked in capital letters, ANTARCTICA.

They got our immediate attention, as they greeted us aloud, "Nice to see you again Mr. and Mrs. Nasser." They were our fellow passengers, from our Antarctic Cruise. I greeted them and thanked them for coming. The lecture was a great success.

Thatcher Private School

I was recommended to Thatcher Private School by Corinne, the parent of a student who had listened to one of my lectures. Thatcher School lies outside of Santa Barbara on beautiful hilly grounds. The administration had arranged for a two night's stay and for me to speak on two occasions. We stayed in the elaborate guest cottage that was reserved for invited individuals for special occasions.

Our host drove us around and showed us the school property. When we got to a large stable full of horses, she explained that in their curriculum, each freshman had a horse assigned to them. They bear the responsibility for the horse's grooming, feeding, and general maintenance. I thought it was a unique approach to teaching responsibility. We ate with the students and after dinner we had my presentation in the new theater. It was full. My son-in-law, Paul, drove up from Chino Hills, California, and we were happy to see him. The audience applauded me and after my book signing, I was surrounded by curious well-wishers. It took me about an hour to get back to our charming guest cottage to rest.

The following day we attended the outdoor theater, a school event. We were seated in the first row. Students came out with a birthday cake with lit candles, and everyone stood up, singing "Happy Birthday". I do not know how they found out that it was my birthday. We left Thatcher with wonderful memories.

Visitors from Canada, 2009

Monique, Françoise's sister, and Blaise, her husband, came down to visit us one summer in Las Vegas. Françoise and I had a week's reservation at our time-share in Laguna Beach. We decided that all four of us should drive to Laguna, stay a week, and continue up the coast toward San Francisco. We had a great time swimming in the ocean. The community and the surrounding area have a lot to offer. We introduced our guests to the Festival of The Arts, an internationally-known annual attraction, with a theatrical staging of masterpiece paintings, created by live performers.

After a week at the time-share, we drove up the Pacific Coast Highway and stayed in motels and enjoyed the beauty that nature has created, like the magnificent scenery of the Pacific Coast. We stopped at Hertz Castle, followed by Solvang, a charming Danish community. We checked into a cozy motel, and the following morning we strolled down Main Street, and had breakfast in a typical Danish bakery and coffee shop. The weather was pleasant, and we enjoyed our two days' stay. The scenic drive to Carmel was enjoyed by all of us. Françoise and I have visited these beautiful spots before. This time it was a different pleasure, because we were able to share the experience with Françoise's family.

In San Francisco we rode the cable cars, visited vibrant China Town, Fisherman's Wharf, Lombard Street, and many other tourist spots. Then we drove inland towards Lake Tahoe where the spectacular lake is surrounded by large gambling casinos. We walked into a casino overlooking the lake, which was a perfect location to celebrate Blaise's 70th birthday. Everyone had a lovely dinner, enjoying the ambiance. As soon as we crossed the California border into Nevada, we were driving beside mountain peaks where Françoise and I had skied many winters before.

We all arrived at Carson City, the capitol of Nevada, and then continued our trip to Virginia City. This historic old mining town charms everyone. We booked passage on an open platform, "mine" train that shows the view of the town as it puffs around the perimeter. We had to wait a couple of hours for the ride, so we just strolled around the wooden sidewalks.

There were some large rocks in one area on the road. To preserve the natural beauty, the wooden walk was cut around these rocks. Suddenly, Françoise tumbled on the rocks, and fell and hit her forehead as she landed face down on the sidewalk and the road. I rushed to comfort her. Blood was running down her cheek. Someone must have called the paramedics. I made sure she had no broken bones before I assisted her in sitting on the sidewalk beside that rock. The paramedics arrived and took over treating Françoise; they cleaned the wound just above the hair line, and started to ask questions. Françoise, being a professional registered nurse, knew the procedure. She cut them off, and said, "My name is Françoise Nasser, I'm a nurse, today's date is...and the President's name is.... AND I'M NOT GOING TO THE HOSPITAL!"

The paramedics had gauze, and some other emergency supplies, but no hydrogen peroxide. I ran from one store to another, pushing my way ahead of tourists, asking desperately for peroxide, explaining the situation. Finally one storekeeper went upstairs and got me a small container. The paramedics cleaned her wound. It was a nasty cut but they managed to stop the bleeding. They recommended ice to keep down the swelling. I ran across the road into a bar, and came back with two thin plastic gloves full of ice cubes. I tied them with a rubber band, as that was the best that I could think of. By now Françoise was sitting on the bench nearby, comforted by her sister. She wasn't too happy to have the loose fingers from the glove hanging down, as we applied the ice.

Françoise looked at her watch and spoke up, "We better hurry, we can't miss the train!"

I didn't think taking the train was a good idea after all that had happened, but we took the train, as Françoise was a "trooper". She sat there on the bench as we took in the sights from the moving railroad car. She still wanted to show her family some other sights, but I "put my foot down", and said that was enough. We drove back to Carson City and got her comfortable in the room. She agreed to stay and rest while the rest of us went out to a restaurant. I brought back dinner for her, and from the drugstore I got some bandages and supplies to change her dressing. On the following day, she insisted on seeing the capitol building.

I was very happy when we got home, and on the following day we went to see her doctor. I was satisfied after the doctor's visit. Françoise recovered, but she had to take it easy for the next few days. Monique and Blaise flew home, mostly with good memories.

Traveling with Good Friends

Our good friend, Ann, devotes, many stress-filled hours to her students, so we all needed some time out. Françoise and I had traveled before in Utah and admired its natural beauty, and had also visited several historical sites that the West has to offer. We decided to share some of the good memories we had previously experienced with Ann and Leigh, so we took advantage of the opportunity when they had a few days off. We drove to Zion and Bryce National Parks. We enjoyed watching their reactions when the panoramic views came into sight. No matter how many times you visit these natural wonders, there is always something new to discover.

We stayed in motels and we were able to leave the everyday stress behind. We also stopped in St. George, Utah for a couple of days. We had reservations at the Tuachan Theater, for two stage presentations. We saw "The Little Mermaid" and "Joseph and the Technicolor Dream Coat"; these plays were world class. The theater was surrounded by magnificent red rock formations, and the huge natural stage is breath-taking. Françoise and I are very familiar with the neighborhood as we have lectured dozens of times in the surrounding communities.

One time we were discussing plans for an unusual New Year's celebration, and we decided to spend it in Death Valley. The hotel, "Death Valley Inn", has seen many Hollywood celebrities in its prime days. It is a high-class, elegant place, surrounded with manicured gardens, a real oasis. To get there, you have to drive through the unforgiving desert landscape, and the other side of the valley, crowned by towering Mount Whitney. We had a fabulous time, and the four of us took many other shorter excursions.

Corinne, Santa Barbara

Corinne, whom I knew from Thatcher Private School, and her husband, invited us the following year. Their two boys were studying in the Santa Barbara area. We stayed with them for a couple of days, and they made us feel at home. Corinne has a show dog named Bijou, a beautiful standard French Poodle. She organized my speaking engagements in the neighborhood. We enjoyed the lovely California community, especially their warm welcome.

Twenty-One

Trip to North Atlantic

Our anniversary was coming up and Françoise and I had a great opportunity to go on a cruise to the North Atlantic. We boarded Holland America Line's *Veendam* in Boston, and sailed to Greenland, the ice-covered continent. We encountered many floating icebergs on our route to Iceland, and we docked at Reykjavik, the capital. This part of the world has lots of volcanic activity. We booked an excursion to the famous Blue Lagoon, which is a geothermal lake, located in a lava field. Françoise and I could hardly wait to dip into the steaming, bluish-green, thermal water. Its temperature varies from 96-102 F. We swam and relaxed in this natural wonder, and stayed as long as we could, without missing our bus returning to the ship.

On board the ship I was approached by the cruise director. "Mr. Nasser, I've information that you are the author of **My Brother's Voice**. Is that correct?'

I answered her, "Yes, it is."

She continued, "Tonight we have our regular stage show, and as it happens, I've a half hour opening just before. Would you be interested in me interviewing you on stage?"

I thought about it for a second; to me it was just another challenge. I replied, "I'll be happy to do it."

That evening Françoise and I entered the theater. We sat in the front row. On stage I saw the plush, floor-to-ceiling curtains, and in front of them two easy chairs, with microphones beside them. The time arrived, and the cruise director accompanied me on stage. After introducing me to the attending audience numbering around 800, she asked me several questions, about my family and origins. She followed up by enquiring about my Concentration Camp experiences, and the diary I'd written there as a young boy. When the interview ended, she announced that because of the shortness of time, I could only answer one question. She choose a person, among many others who raised their hands.

He stood up and spoke, "I lived in Holland during the war, near the railroad. From the front of my house, I saw Jews being taken away. Sometimes they banged on my window desperately. I'm on a cruise now, and I don't want to listen to all this nonsense!"

The cruise director was standing beside my chair, holding onto her mike with a worried expression on her face. Her eyes were focused on me. I sat calmly and answered without any hesitation, "Sir, you are entitled to your opinion. Nobody forced you to listen to this interview. So, now it is my turn to answer. I've stated this a few times before. I refuse to let my mind sink into the gutter, where yours is. Even if you do not believe that the Holocaust happened, it is your problem. Whenever you are willing to face reality, without anger in your heart, give me a call, and then we can have an intelligent conversation. Now, go in peace and have a great life."

The audience rose to their feet applauding. After the show I was surrounded as people wanted to shake my hand and talk to me. In the lineup was the man with the attitude. When he got to me he said, "Sir, I didn't mean my comment the way it sounded."

I replied without any anger, "I heard you clearly. God bless you and have a good life." I shook his extended hand, and turned to the person following him.

In the days to follow, I had many questions from fellow passengers, as lots of them wanted to read my book. One night at dinner time, I took a private moment to glance upwards and thought, *"Andris! I hope you are with us. I'm sure you are sharing our smiles, as we are enjoying life!"*

I lifted my glass and told Françoise, "Let's have a toast, for the ones who cannot be with us." She looked in my eyes, and knew me well enough to understand as we clinked glasses.

I thought, "Life is beautiful. Enjoying life to the fullest and still keeping my promise to my brother, with all the lectures and book signings behind us and only God knows what's ahead of us. There is no way I could have done all this alone; Françoise is an equal partner, and without her help and encouragement, I could never have gone this far."

The rest of the cruise was relaxing, as we visited Holland, Norway, Greenland, and Newfoundland. It was nice to get home again, and have some time to catch up with our paperwork and prepare for future speaking engagements.

Las Vegas High School

Don, a highly dedicated teacher from Las Vegas High School, invited us again to speak to the students. As I entered the large theater, to my surprise it was already filled to capacity. I was standing beside the podium, and Don was making the introduction. I sensed something unusual as the principal, accompanied by another teacher, joined us.

The principal took the microphone and said, "Today we have a special presentation for Mr. Nasser. For years he has been speaking all over the world, spreading the importance of family values and freedom, and today is his 700th lecture. Mr. Nasser and his brother Andris, who died in his arms in the concentration camp, had no chance to graduate from high school. The administration of Las Vegas High School has decided to give Mr. Nasser two Honorary Graduation Certificates, honoring him and his beloved brother."

At that moment, I was given a large framed plaque with the two certificates and a golden honor cord and a heartwarming poem, written by the teacher standing beside us. There were calls from the audience, for me to read the poem that was presented to me.

The teacher responded and read the poem:

"Boys of Courage"
"Two young boys with life to live,
Two young boys with love to give,
Always clinging to each other,
They lived their lives brother to brother.
One life gone with days too few,
The other telling what he once knew.
He shares his story of struggle and strife,
Touching hearts as he tells of each life.
Their pain of days swallowed up in love,
As they put their faith in God above.
No high school diploma until today,
As we honor the boys in a special way.
What two young boys have earned,
We now give for what we've learned.
We've learned that hatred strips the soul,
We've learned some stories must be told.
We've learned to love and forgive,
We've learned a better way to live."

I could not keep my emotions under control, as I said, "This is the greatest honor I could receive. Thank you for this poem, it must have come from your heart." I lifted the plaque skyward, and said, "Andris this is for both of us, you are not beside me, but you are locked in my heart, until we meet again."

I don't think there were too many dry eyes in the audience. I lost control and tears ran down my cheeks. Françoise rushed over and hugged me. The audience rose to their feet in my honor. I swallowed deeply and cleared my throat. Nothing could stop me from delivering my message. I can never forget that moment!

The following day, we attended Don's Holocaust Museum. He annually creates this unbelievable achievement. It takes him many days of hard work to put together this exhibit, mostly by himself; however, a small handful of students do help him. The museum contains many plaques, articles, pictures and memorabilia he has collected throughout the years. Don kept it open just for a few days to commemorate the anniversary of the Holocaust. I have been invited to this annual event ever since he organized it.

Guadalajara, Mexico

A couple of years ago, I had met a gentleman by the name of Jose in Budapest on a river cruise. I received an email from Guadalajara, Mexico, from Jose inviting Françoise and me to speak to an audience. We had a good friend, Elfie, and her associate, Beatrice who wanted to join us. They took care of their own arrangements and we stayed at the same hotel. Jose picked us up at the airport, and drove us to our hotel. He pre-purchased books and every guest had a chance to read it in advance. He widely advertised the event and sent out many flyers. There was a dinner reception in the hotel. It was open to the public, by reservation only. The following day was the big event.

During the day all four of us went sightseeing. We got back in time to clean up and had a sit-down dinner in the hotel. Half an hour before starting, we checked the projection and sound system, and everything was in order. The invited guests wore a hearing device. In the back of the auditorium, there was a professional translator in a glass enclosure. He continuously translated my complete lecture from English to Spanish. I was surprised by the skill of this translator. I started out speaking slowly; to give him a chance to do his job and soon he signaled me to speak at my normal speed. It was a great success.

The following night, all six of us went to see a dinner show, in a Mexican folk-lore theater. Jose and his girlfriend accompanied us. It was a trip and lecture I will remember for a long time. All four of us flew home with great memories.

Upland Library

In California we were invited to speak at the Library of Upland to the general public. The librarian advertised my speech in local papers and flyers. Françoise and I decided to get there somewhat earlier. When we arrived, attendants were changing signs from the pre-assigned meeting room to a much larger room. We met the librarian and she explained to us that there were so many inquires that they had decided to change my lecture to their largest auditorium. I set up my power point. When we arrived, there were at least forty or more people seated in the meeting room. I saw Paul, my son-in-law arriving, and we greeted each other.

Paul remarked, "There is a big crowd in line outside."

From the podium, I noticed that people kept coming in from both entrances. Soon all of the chairs were taken, and many people decided to stand against the side walls. I was introduced and I took the microphone. I began to share my experiences with the 400+ people in the audience.

Françoise and I were the last to leave the auditorium and Paul informed us, "While you were talking, there were lots of unhappy people who were refused entry and missed your lecture. The police had to be summoned, to have the crowd peacefully dispersed. I felt bad for the people, but I was glad that there were no injuries.

Twenty-Two

PUBLISHING MY BOOK IN GERMANY

An old friend, Leonard, of Palm Springs, introduced Heinz Bickert of Schwalmstadt, Germany to us. We had met him in Las Vegas, just outside the Golden Nugget Hotel. Heinz was a retired teacher and he spoke excellent English. We developed a warm relationship with Heinz despite the short time we spent with him. He flew back to Germany, taking *My Brother's Voice* with him. We kept in touch with him through casual emails.

One day, to our surprise, Heinz wrote to us explaining how the book had affected him, and that he had decided to translate it into German. We negotiated with Heinz, but he was determined; he wanted no monetary benefit from the book. He maintained that the book was written so well that it led the reader into the Camps, reliving the reality, just the way it had happened. Heinz started to search for a publisher and his perseverance paid off. He got a commitment from Wolfgang of Austria. I negotiated with them through email. In Las Vegas we had met Albert Marquis, a well-known attorney, and through him, we met Attorney Bryon Harding who specialized in contracts. Through Bryan's generosity, we obtained a signed contract from Wolfgang. He published the German version of my book, *Die Stimme meines Bruthers* (*My Brother's Voice*).

Walter Steffen a film Maker, from Seeshaupt, Germany, (the town I was liberated from on April 30, 1945) contacted us. Walter explained to me that he was ready to release a documentary film based on Muhldorf Concentration Camp. He was very disappointed that he had known nothing about my book and me, before he produced the documentary. He did read the German version of my book after his documentary, *End Station Seeshaupt*, was completed. He planned to have the film released in many theaters, in and around Munich, Muhldorf, Seeshaupt, and several other communities. Since the official release of **Die Stimme meines Bruders** coincided with the release of his documentary, Heinz and Walter organized a trip for Françoise and me to be available for the premiere introduction of the film and the book.

Heinz drove an hour and a half from his house to the Frankfurt Airport, where he picked us up at around 7:30 A.M. It was a sunny day, and his Mercedes smoothly sailed by the charming countryside. I asked Heinz if I could help him with the driving. He had a smile on his face, as he assured me he was doing just fine. It took us several hours to reach the outskirts of Muhldorf, where my former Concentration Camp used to be. Heinz drove very slowly, to give me a chance to turn back the pages of my memory. I concentrated very hard on spotting our former Camp site. I felt we had arrived at the approximate location of the old camp site on the left side of the road. Now, it was built up and looked like a subdivision. I thought about how people live on the same ground, under totally different circumstances from Andris and me, who with others had to struggle day-to-day for our survival.

On the right side of the road, the thick pine forest was still untouched. Then we came to the Inn River, which brought back many devastating memories of bygone times. I knew soon after passing the river that we should be entering Muhldorf. I had a hard time recognizing the city's main street as it had changed through the years. In my memory, there used to be an old bakery and a butcher shop, that our Nazi captors had forced us to march by. I believe that the bakery we drove by was the same bakery, but in 66 years, a lot had changed.

We checked into a small hotel where we stayed for bed and breakfast with Heinz. The following day we had a reception across the street in a large hall. We met Edwin Hamberger who had helped to make our visit possible. Then Wolgang Hasere, a reporter from *Muhldorfer Anzeiger*, interviewed us. It was a busy day! After asking many questions, Hans drove us to a memorial for Holocaust victims and also to the mass grave where I believed my brother Andris was buried. It was a day full of emotion for me.

After Muhldorf we drove to Seeshaupt, where we checked into a small hotel with Heinz. There we met up with one of our hosts, Walter Steffen the filmmaker. He had a very busy schedule set up for us. Walter had a good-sized SUV and he zipped across the well-built German autobahns, the super highways that have no speed limits. We had our safety belts secured, and got used to Walter's heavy foot on the gas paddle.

I even remarked, "Walter, I don't know how fast you are going, but the other speeding cars beside us, look like they are driving backwards!"

Walter answered, with a sense of humor, "We are not driving, we are flying low! We have many presentations to attend. We have three to four theaters to stop by, and many more in the next several days. Just hang on!" He spoke loudly, as we sped on, leaving other vehicles behind.

We developed a routine. The documentary was an hour and a half long. Before the film started, Walter introduced me in German, and spoke about my book. Then we had a table set up with a spotlight attached. I was sitting at the table with Walter's fourteen-year-old son, Daniel, and I read a short

Daniel and Pista reading to a German audience.

pre-selected portion of my book in English, and then his son read the same from the German book.

After we finished, they rolled the film.

All five of us, Walter, his son, Daniel, Heinz, Françoise and I, drove quickly to a local eatery where we grabbed a bite and returned to the theater. In the lobby we had **Stimme meines Bruders** displayed for sale. When the crowed came out, I signed the books. This routine we repeated on many occasions. During these presentations, for the first time I met the publisher, Wofgang Maxilmoser. I also noticed a German woman accompanied by a gentleman. She introduced herself as Milena Finus and he, as Wolfgangn Bechtel. She was very friendly and complimentary toward us, mentioning something about "Stolpersteins". Heinz explained that Milena is involved with an organization that promotes and places memorial stones for families murdered by the Nazis.

He said, "Don't think about it now, but it could happen in the future."

We kept on with our presentations, not having too much rest, and we became friendly with Milena, and had many conversations with her. After we had finished presenting the documentary, we had some individual presentations in Seeshaupt. With Heinz we drove to Dachau, and spent a few hours there, viewing the gas chamber and the crematorium. I was interviewed and videotaped. We continued driving, following the route of the "Death Train".

We stopped at a city called Poing where we found a memorial sculpture created by an artist, displaying bronze figures rushing forward. Heinz asked me, "Does this place bring back memories to you?'

I answered, "I remember about 66 years ago. They put us on a so-called "Death Train".

It originated in Muhldorf, my former prison camp. I remembered we stopped at Poing, where we heard a powerful voice screaming, "Alles Frei!" ("Everybody Free!") The doors opened, and any of the prisoners who were able to, started to abandon the train. I was too weak to move, as I was undernourished, just bare skin and bones. I was lying helplessly on the floor of the cattle car, and struggled to pull myself closer to the door's edge. I saw prisoners rushing toward the village of Poing. Some were running, others were limping and barely moving, but most everyone was getting away from the "Death Train", toward freedom. But, it was a false alarm. The Nazis still had a foothold in the village. The S.S. with their rifles and guns were firing at the helpless prisoners. I just laid there in terror, watching my fellow prisoners being killed like fish in a barrel."

After my explanation to Heinz about what had happened there many years ago, we visited the memorial erected to these victims. The Burgermeister was present, and addressed the crowd as Françoise and I stood solemnly beside the monument. I felt lucky to be alive, and not to have been one of the victims.

Heinz wanted to show us some of the scenery of Bavaria, and we stopped at Oberammergau. This lovely Bavarian village is world known, hosting the "Passion Play". We continued our sightseeing, and ended up in Schwalmstadt. Heinz and his wife Marita, and their daughter Sabrina, live in this charming village. He took us to a local hotel and dropped us off to have a chance to relax and refresh. He was going to pick us up later and welcome us for dinner at his home. As we entered his house through an impressive stairway, we were greeted by the sounds of two dogs, followed by three people. Heinz introduced us to his wife, Marita, daughter, Sabrina and friend, Marko. We all had a delicious homemade dinner. Sabrina explained that she takes her dog to her classes at the high school while she teaches. The students treated the dog as a mascot.

On the following day, Heinz arranged for us to meet all of his friends, for dinner in a typical Bavarian Restaurant. These people helped in finalizing *Die Stimme meines Bruders*, before it went into printing,

Sabrina had invited us to speak at the high school, where she teaches. (Her dog was quietly lying on a rug underneath a small table.) I spoke for an hour to the German students and we did not need an interpreter, because, to my surprise, they understood English. Before we left Schwalmstadt, Heinz introduced us to the Burgermeister. The following morning he was kind enough to drive us to Frankfurt Airport, for our flight back to Las Vegas.

Back Home in Las Vegas

In July 2012, my son-in-law Paul asked me to be the best man at his upcoming wedding to June, an English lady. The ceremony was held in Chino, California, followed by a reception at Paul's home. It was a very nice reception, but I could not help to think back, to my daughter, Michele's wedding in 1984. I accept the fact that we cannot alter history, and Françoise and I wished the new couple a pleasant life.

Thanksgiving dinners have been a tradition at our house in Las Vegas. Chelsea, June and Paul stay over for a few days. A couple of times we also invited good friends of ours, Elfie and her son Steven, to join our family dinner. Françoise and I stay at Chino Hills, with Paul and June, usually in January as we are invited by the schools in their area. Chelsea has a condo in La Jolla and an apartment in Hollywood where she lives to be close to her profession of photography. We are all very proud of her.

Back in Las Vegas, I got an email from the parents of a California student. Their daughter had read my book and would love to meet me in Las Vegas. This would be a present for her birthday, and I agreed to meet them. Françoise and I met the family at "Tommy Bahama" restaurant, where we spent a couple of hours together. They were very friendly and genuinely interested to meet with me. The mother asked me, "Mr. Nasser, I have been told that you have a special way to make the students realize the importance of family. Could you shed some light on how you accomplish that?"

I bent toward them, and said, "I get their attention by saying, Look into my eyes. I've lost 20 people in my family. I would give one half of my life, to be able to give my brother, mother, and father a hug! But I can't.

They have been murdered by Nazi bullies. But most of you people still have some loved ones at home. Every family needs a hero. I challenge you to go home, and give a big hug to your family members, and tell them 'I love you'. This will be an unexpected, but great present to them. You will be rewarded by a warm feeling running through your soul. And if you have enough guts, give them a second hug, and let them know that this hug is from Mr. Nasser, because he hasn't got a chance to hug his family." My guests were speechless. The mother stood up and gave me a warm hug. A short while later we departed and we all embraced one another.

We do our best to communicate with people. We respect their families and in turn we earn their respect. This message I've delivered to more than 200,000 people. During the year, I receive many requests to answer or to give advice. When the request is a phone call or email, I do my best to answer.

Stolpersteins, September 28, 2012

I had received emails and telephone calls from Milena in Germany. She reminded me of the "Stolperstein Project" (memorial brass plaques), she had mentioned when we met at my book presentation last year in Germany. She explained that the Project would take place, if Françoise and I would fly to Budapest on September 28, 2012, and we came to an agreement. Milena explained that she and Wolfgang wanted to be present when the German artist, Gunther Damnig, would install the six memorial plaques called "Stolpersteins" into the sidewalk in front of the house where I was born.

I started to make plane reservations and searched on the computer for a hotel near transportation. I found just the spot that I thought was in a good location, and Milena requested that I book a place for them in the same hotel. We arrived at the hotel and met Milena and Wolfgang on September 27th. On the 28th, all four of us took the subway, and from the station it was a short walk to Arpad St.

42. We got there three-quarters of an hour early. As we were crossing the street, we saw the Nasser house and two uniformed policemen standing in front.

The Nasser House where the family was deported from to the Concentration Camp.

We looked at each other, and the same thought occurred to us; the police were there to stop the installation of the plaques. We were dead wrong as the police were assigned for our protection.

We were the first ones to arrive, so I showed Milena and Wolfgang the house the Nassers used to own since 1872. While we were conversing, a large van with a German license plate pulled up. Gunther Damnig, the artist and his associates, arrived in front of the house. We all introduced ourselves. The two men had brought a diamond-gritted cement saw, and all kinds of other equipment. We had an official permit allowing the artist to cut into the sidewalk in front of the entrance to the house, authorized by the Hungarians. While Gunther connected to electric power, several more people arrived, including my cousin's son, Tamas, a good friend from the U.S., Eugene, the Mayor of the city, a film crew, and several local bystanders.

The saw cut into the cement, screeching and throwing bright sparks into the air. Gunther has installed many of these "Stolpersteins" in other European cities, so he knew what he was doing. There were six plaques dedicated: one each to my Dad, Dezso, Mom, Eugenia, Aunt Bozsi, cousin, Peter, my brother, Andris, and myself, Istvan. Milena laid fresh flowers beside the plaques.

There was a short ceremony, during which I tried to control my emotions and some of my tears. I just knew that from above I had my loved ones with me, at least in my heart.

In the days to follow we spent time together with our German friends, as we introduced them to the sights and

The Stolpersteins. Memorial Plaques, for the Nasser Family.

sounds of Budapest. Finally, it was time to say goodbye to Milena and Wolfgang. They never acknowledged it, but we knew that they were the ones who had made this honor to my family a reality. Milena and Wolfgang flew back to Germany.

Françoise and I stayed a few more days. We visited my old high school, "Konyves Kalman Gimnazium". The impressive building looked in excellent shape. I met the principal and I asked her if there was a chance that the school had any trace of me or my brother Andris attending the school. She walked over to a floor-to-ceiling book shelf and stepped onto an attached sliding wooden ladder, and to my amazement; she got a large book from the crowded shelves, and found my brother Andris's and my grades from the 1942/43 school year. To top it off, she also showed as an impressive hardcover book of the 1905-2005 millennium edition of the school's history.

I asked her, "Where can I buy a book like this?"

She replied, "Unfortunately it is out of print." I felt her eyes watching my reaction and then she sported a big smile, "Mr. Nasser, this book belongs to you, it is yours to keep." I was overwhelmed. I'm very proud to have that book, as it is very precious to me. It found a permanent home in our living room in Las Vegas.

Before returning to the U.S, we visited my cousin Daisy who was 91 years old. Daisy wanted to make us a nice, home-cooked dinner. After she agreed that we could help her prepare the meal, we cooked, and then we all sat down and enjoyed our Hungarian feast. After dinner she shared with us some family pictures. I made a comment, "It is lucky you still have so many photographs."

Daisy replied, "If it wasn't for Raul Wallenberg, I wouldn't have the pictures and we wouldn't be alive. When the Nazis took your family and my parents in 1944 from the outskirts of Ujpest, we were lucky in the inner city. We were able to get Swedish passports and found refuge in the so-called Swedish safe houses established by Raul Wallenberg. He saved 24,000 Hungarian Jews."

At the table we shared the pictures, re-living old times. Daisy gave me a few more of the old photographs to keep. In the corner of the room I noticed something familiar. I asked Daisy, "Is that the old globe of the world that used to be at Uncle Bela's office?"

She was surprised, "Yes it is! How do you know?"

When I lived with Aunt Manci and Uncle Bela, that globe was on his desk in the large room I used to sleep in. It holds many pleasant memories of Vera and me as we studied that globe before I immigrated to Canada. It meant a lot to me as I have nothing left from Vera. "Do you think I could have it?" I asked with a deep sigh.

"Of course, Pistukam, but how can you take it with you? It is too large for the plane!"

I replied, "Klara will arrive next week from Baltimore, perhaps she could help and mail it to me. Of course, I will cover all expenses." (Klara, Daisy's daughter was very good to her and she visited very often.) In a few weeks, I had the globe in our house, the only physical reminder I had left of Vera.

We had a very busy week there, but accomplished a lot. The following day we checked out of our hotel and flew back to Las Vegas.

Original Globe Vera and Pista viewed, before departed to Canada..

Twenty-Three

Trip to Washington and Montreal

The year was 2013, the place, Washington D. C. The Jewish Federation had arranged a huge get-together, honoring Holocaust Survivors. It was the 20th anniversary of the Holocaust Museum, originally opened by President Clinton and Ellie Wiesel.

Our good friend, Elfie from Las Vegas joined us again. We all made our reservations way ahead, and the three of us checked into the hotel.

Elie Wiesel and Pista.

We did some sightseeing, and attended the festivities in a huge tent, just next to the Holocaust Museum. There were close to 3000 attendees seated around elegantly-set tables, ready for a gala dinner including wine. The food was excellent.

After dinner we relaxed and made

friends with the people sitting around us. Soon the lights dimmed, the stage was lit, and we were waiting for the celebrities to appear. Everybody stood up applauding when former President Bill Clinton and Elie Wiesel were introduced as the keynote speakers. There were huge television screens visible from all angles. Many other dignitaries were introduced, and we listened to all of them.

Afterwards we returned to our hotel, and the following day we visited the Holocaust Museum. It includes the history and events that led up to the Holocaust; the Nazi brutality including the cooperation of the satellite countries were well documented. We then visited the library, and spoke to the librarian, who showed me the shelf where my book, *My Brother's Voice*, was part of their huge collection.

We stayed for two nights, and then Françoise and I flew to Montreal to visit her family. Elfie flew on to visit some of her friends. After arriving in Montreal, Canada, we rented a car and drove to Mt. St. Hillarie where Liliane, her daughter, Marie Claude, husband, Alain, and two children, Jean Philip, Vincent and their French poodle, Maya, lived in their newly remodeled house. It was a great re-union. Just a few months before, while Françoise and I were traveling, we had gotten disturbing news from Canada, we had almost lost Liliane. She was out of the hospital now and recovering rapidly at home, under the constant care of her loved ones. The new house was spacious and well-designed. Liliane had her old comfort, which she was used to, and the new upstairs addition had enough privacy for the parents and boys. The large back garden became a mini resort, when they added a spacious swimming pool. We spent a few restful days with the family. Monique, Blaize, and Sophie joined us from Québec City. We flew back to Las Vegas, knowing that Liliane was well cared for.

Laguna Vacation with Friends

Every year we make reservations to stay in our timeshare in Laguna Beach, in the three- storied, brick structure overlooking the beach. Each unit has a bedroom with its private bath, and a large combination sitting room with a fireplace, a dining area, and a complete kitchen with appliances. Cleverly folded into the wall is a comfortable Murphy-bed for two people. The condo also had a second bathroom with a dressing area sealed behind a door. From the sitting room, we stepped out onto a large balcony, with a table and four chairs, and a good-sized gas barbeque to take care of our appetites. Below the patio spread the wide, sandy beach, washed by the constant surf of the blue Pacific. We took a staircase going down from our resort, right onto the white sandy beach.

Ann and Leigh and we live in Las Vegas, so we picked them up and drove about 300 miles to the time share. By the time we arrived and unpacked, we were all in a holiday mood. We did our grocery shopping and prepared a quick snack, and then relaxed on the patio. Sea gulls were flying behind us, occasionally settling on the railing. Some of them were brave enough to take food from our extended hands. The following day we walked to the village's main street and strolled down it, doing some window-shopping.

Ann and I tossed around the idea of writing a stage play, with the name of *Not Yet, Pista*. The title came from a memory dating back to 1945, when I was unconscious during the liberation and I was hallucinating and thought I saw my brother Andris in Heaven. I wanted to stay with him, but he firmly said, *"Not yet, Pista."* We both worked very hard on writing the script, and we decided the starting point would be the Stolpersteins in front of the old Nasser House. It took us over a year to write it, but we have completed the script. We do have a stage manager, Maggie, who has volunteered to help us to produce the play on stage. We are searching for financial support. When it is all completed, Humanity will benefit from the message, carrying it on to future generations. We all must recognize the importance of respecting family, appreciating freedom, and reducing the harm caused by bullies in our society. We safely got back from Laguna, in time to fulfill our upcoming commitments.

Upland 2013 Chaffey High School

This was my third invitation from Chaffey High School in Upland, California. I always have an excellent reception there. They gave me one and a half hours for my presentation. When I got up on the stage, I knew we had a large audience of around 700 people. I do not use notes to speak. As soon as I have the microphone in my hand, mentally I step back into the past and make the audience a participant in my surroundings. At the conclusion of the speaking engagement, I left the stage and joined Françoise sitting below waiting for me to sign the books. I had difficulty getting to my chair beside her, as crowds of people, mainly students, were waiting to shake my hands and give me hugs, boys and girls alike. Finally I was sitting and signing books. I could have used more lights overhead, but I managed to read the names I had to write and sign on the book's title page. We did not have much breathing space because of the crowd surrounding us.

One young man, a few feet away, was trying to get my attention, looking over the shoulders of other students. "Mr. Nasser, Mr. Nasser. I have something important to tell you!

You remember back in Muhldorf Concentration Camp, you gave a carving of a horse's head to a Wermacht soldier and he gave you two pencils as you requested? He was my grandfather."

People who heard the comment and had read my book previously, looked at me with amazement. I was shocked. I wanted to ask many questions. A shiver ran down my spine as I quickly remembered the episode 70 years ago. I was just sitting there, with a pen in my hand. I jumped to my feet, but the young man was gone.

Meeting Governor Sandoval

Françoise and I got an invitation from the Jewish Family Services, sponsored by Sheldon Edelson and his wife, Miriam. They provided the services of their private jet, to fly us to Carson City, to attend Yam Hashoa commemoration services, honoring the Holocaust. The event was hosted by the Governor of Nevada, Biron Sandoval.

We met in the morning at the Executive Terminal in Las Vegas; there were about 30 of us, with our spouses. The Edelson's private crew welcomed us like royalty. I had never flown first class, but this was "A Class-fit for a King"! There were no aisles, just seats on both sides. The jet's interior was arranged like a sitting room, with plush leather chairs and sofas, with tables scattered around the cabin covered with scrumptious appetizers and beverages. We didn't have to ring for service as stewardesses surrounded us. We landed at the Reno Airport and were bussed into Carson City, where we disembarked at the Governor's Mansion. We were seated on rows of chairs set up in the large reception hall. All of us survivors had nametags identifying our seats, while the spouses sat separately.

Governor Sandoval welcomed us all. We had a small ceremony, and a choir singing set the atmosphere. A long table covered with a white tablecloth was set up with candles to be lit. Several of us survivors were pre-selected to light the memorial candles as we were called up and then stayed there until the ceremony finished.

Afterward, we had a buffet of great selections of cold cuts and fruit. There was plenty of time to answer questions, as we mixed with the dignitaries. I gave Governor Sandoval an autographed copy of *My Brother's Voice* and a sample of my recently completed play, *Not Yet, Pista*, as we posed for photographers.

We flew home the same day with unforgettable memories.

Pista handing his play, Not Yet, Pista, to Governor Sandoval.

Busy Schedule Ahead

In 2014 our calendar filled up very quickly with invitations to many schools. In January I spoke to the Mesquite Club, here in Las Vegas. A few days later we drove to Chino Hills, California, to fulfill about twelve speaking engagements at schools and libraries. We stayed at my son-in-law, Paul's place. When we're in California, we never rest. Usually I have two speaking engagements per day, each lasting about one and a half hours. Françoise and I try to have a starting time around 9:00 A.M. whenever possible. Sometimes the school calendar requires us to start as early as 7:30 a.m. We have to arrive half an hour earlier to set up my power point presentation. At times like that we have to get up early, around 5:30 A.M. We are not youngsters any more, as I'm over 80, and trying to enjoy the "Golden Age." However nobody told me that "gold tarnishes" and it can be very uncomfortable. This "minor" setback does not stop us from keeping my promise to my brother, Andris.

After the California tour, we drove back to Las Vegas and had less than a week to recover. Following up on our next commitments, we drove to Arizona. Our first stop is usually Sedona, with its breathtaking, red rock formations. Annually we visit schools in Cottonwood and Cornville. Than we drive on to Dewey, Mayer, Prescott Valley, and Prescott. From Prescott we drive to Glendale. We spoke at the school in Surprise, where we met up with a couple who were sitting at our dinner table on a previous cruise. What a small world! From there we continued to Phoenix, El Mirage, Peoria, and Wickenburg.

Returning to Las Vegas, we had just a few days to rest until we were on the road again to St. George, Utah. While in St George, Suzy and Chuck always lay out the welcome mat with their friendship. Their family is the living example of love. We have met their family on several occasions. Staying at their lovely home is like relaxing in an oasis, before starting the lectures. We have been invited by many schools in St. George over the past eight years; five schools within the city and two schools in the community of Hurricane.

January, February, March and April are our busiest times for speaking engagements, although we have several calls during the year. It is a welcome relief, when annually we can spend some free time in Laguna Beach at our time share. After driving thousands of miles and lecturing at many institutions, we are ready for some well-earned relaxation. For our anniversary and Françoise and my birthdays, we booked a special treat.

Twenty-Four

SOUTH AMERICAN ADVENTURE

Françoise and I flew to Rio, the city of carnivals, and stayed in a hotel overlooking Copa Cabana Beach. This international city has many world famous landmarks. We took the cable car to Sugar Loaf Mountain and enjoyed the breathtaking view below us, the blue Pacific with its wide curved sandy beach of Copa Cabana. The row of hotels and large buildings followed the curvature of the beach. As we left our hotel and walked toward the popular summer haven, we could not miss the striped beauty of Portuguese pebbled walks artfully contrasting with the sand. The slender, sky-reaching palms give it a finishing touch. It was an unforgettable view from Sugar Loaf. Looking in another direction, we saw another world famous landmark, Christ the Redeemer Statue, on Corcovado Mountain.

Francoise and Stephen in Rio Brazil.

Our next port of call was Buenos Aires, the capital of Argentina, where we stayed two nights in the city of "Evita". We wanted to see Iguassu Falls, so we took a short flight and had a once-in-a-lifetime experience seeing the most majestic falls of any falls we had seen before (Niagara and Victoria Falls). There is an Argentinean and a Brazilian side to the Falls and since we had an excellent guide, we saw both. They spread many miles, and the tiers of cascades, with the mist rising from the rushing waters, were breath-taking. Returning to the city, we visited the grave of Evita, and had time to marvel at an Argentinean Tango Club.

We visited the Falkland Islands, and saw lots of war-torn landscapes. We sailed south to Tierra del Fuego and Cape Horn. We docked at Ushuaia and saw many snow covered mountains as we turned north following the Chilean coast. We docked in Valparaiso, and mixed with the locals at the market place, and then continued sailing north to Lima, Peru. The people there were very friendly; we bought some Alpaca sweaters, and hand-made artifacts.

Cusco and Machu Pichu

Next, we took an hour long flight to Cusco, with an elevation of 11,150 feet, our jumping-off point by train to Machu Picchu. These Inca ruins are a UNESCO World Heritage site. The train trip from Cusco was an experience, after boarding the train; we went back and forth, switching tracks, climbing higher and higher. Finally the train reached the main track to Machu Pichu. It was a panoramic and exhilarating ride, until we arrived at the base of the Inca Enclave. We stayed in a very nice, comfortable bungalow for two nights.

The day of the adventurous bus ride arrived, and on very primitive roads, our bus climbed many switchbacks, until we reached our final destination. This was another life experience. The city was built in the 15th century and mysteriously abandoned. After visiting many buildings, Françoise and I decided to hike up to the Gate of the Sun. Taking the original Inca trail, we followed very narrow passes, with several hundred feet drops, below us most of the time. I went sideways, hugging the mountain as I didn't dare to look behind me. I do have a phobia although Françoise is not bothered by heights, so she was good company.

Finally we made it to our destination and the view was unbelievable. At the Gate of the Sun were some "safe" flat surfaces to stand upon.

I had a great time taking pictures, and not thinking about facing my returning trip. But I made it! Françoise was proud of me for overcoming my fear of heights.

After returning to Cusco, we took a thirty minute flight to the tributaries of the mighty Amazon, where we stayed in a very primitive jungle lodge. We slept in a large, wooden barrack divided into smaller sleeping compartments, with twin beds covered by mosquito nets. The room also held a free-standing wooden dresser, and on top was an enameled wash bowl with a pitcher of water. There was no washroom and no electricity for the cabins, so we used candles and flashlights. The community wash-

Francoise and Stephen at Gate of the Sun, Machu Picchu.

rooms were housed in a separate structure, a few hundred feet away from our sleeping quarters. We had to walk through the jungle terrain to use the facility, and at night that was an adventure. Without the moon it was pitch dark, except for the scattered containers of small oil cans supplying flickering dim light, leading to the toilets. The shower was built over the river and a wooden walk led to it. When we showered, the water was pumped from the river below, at river water's temperature. I personally enjoyed roughing it.

Our guides took us fishing for piranhas on a small motorboat. Since the area was over a flooded jungle terrain, we had to duck as we worked our way through trees and large bushes protruding from the water. Françoise caught a piranha, and they cooked it for her that same night. The following day we went on a hike through the jungle; our destination was a tree-top walk. There was one massive tree with wooden stairs attached all around the trunk, inching their way above to the canopy of the forest. We could not see the sky from the ground below, because the branches were so thick. We climbed many steps around the tree, and finally we were at tree-top level, way above the ground. We had company on the way up as playful monkeys were jumping from limb to limb and colorful parrots sailed above, settling on nearby branches, making an ear- shattering racket. We were spectators outnumbered in nature's paradise. There were rope bridges connecting high above ground. We could cross only one at a time, from tree top to tree top. Humidity took its toll, affecting even the best of us; we were perspiring from the steaming jungle. It was an experience we will never forget.

The last day we visited a primitive native village where we learned that there are places untouched by modern life, where people are living in very substandard conditions. They are human beings, with their families, and enjoying life as they know it. We distributed some gifts to them, but their gifts to us were much more valuable with warmth and friendship coming from their hearts. We continued our trip to Quito, Ecuador where we did some sightseeing before we left for the Galapagos Islands. There we followed in the footsteps of Darwin as on our first day we explored the giant turtles. Then we boarded a small boat and cruised from island to island, and each time we landed, a new adventure waited for us. We encountered Galapagos penguins, blue and red footed Boobies, and land iguanas. We snorkeled in the Bay of Seals, and came face to face underwater with several playful sea lions. On the beach we had to keep our distance from the sea lions, as they were extremely protective over their young pups.

During our adventures I could not help reminiscing about the past. Close to starvation, beaten, Andris and I relied on each other's support. How have I deserved such a fantastic life, leaving my family behind? Then I imagined Andris' smiling face, repeating, *"You kept your promise, we are proud of you!"* Occasions like that brought tears to my eyes.

Francoise and Stephen at the Galapagos after snorkeling with sea lyons.

Françoise's Injury

By the time we returned to Las Vegas, we had a lot of emails to answer, and requests for speaking engagements. I had no doubt in my mind that I had to go on, and fulfill all the requests.

I was concerned about Françoise, since she fell a couple of years ago, after lecturing, while leaving a school in Prescott, Arizona. She had taken a wrong step and landed on her left hip. I had helped her to stand and she assured me, "Don't worry, I'm O.K.!"

"Let's go to a hospital and have it checked!" I replied.

But she walked away without any difficulties. A couple of days later she had trouble walking. Since then years have gone by. She has been examined by an orthopedic specialist, had an MRI, and several x-rays. The results were all negative, so we just had to learn how to adjust. My walk has slowed down too, because of my age. We became each other's support. Keeping my promise to Andris has become a challenge for us, to get around, to speak in different cities and states.

"If I survived the Concentration Camp, nothing can slow me down!" I thought.

I do have to worry about Françoise. It is upsetting to see her in pain, with no hope of getting any relief. As we are getting older, we have decided to take some pleasure trips while we are still able to. Cruises are more our speed now. We relax if want to, and participate only in some physical activities. These excursions rejuvenate us, and give us enough hope, to keep on speaking, and fulfilling my promise to my brother. Eventually, we will have to stop traveling and delivering my personal message to the public. I did plan for this phase of life, as I have a DVD available with my 60 minute, professionally recorded message. The video can be presented, whenever I'm not able to speak any more. However, I hope I can still make myself available for book signing or question and answers period. Also, we have written the script for the play, *Not Yet, Pista* for stage or movie screen, with the help of my good friend, Ann. This play will deliver my message to Humanity, even after I join my beloved family. I'm also writing a manuscript, soon to be published as a book, ***Journey to Freedom.*** I have had thousands of requests from former readers of **My Brother's Voice** and lecture attendees, who wanted to know how my life progressed after I left Hungary following the Holocaust.

Françoise and I always find refuge in the comfort of our home in Las Vegas, whether we are returning from a lecture tour, or a planned vacation. Our gated community offers us all that we have dreamed of. We have tennis courts, swimming pools, a club house, and a golf course. We have played a lot of tennis with each other, and doubles with our friends whenever they stayed with us. We always have a good time in their company. Our life has readjusted, to a different speed. But, despite getting older, Françoise and I carry on our mission to speak.

Since my quintuple bypass heart surgery, I have not had any major medical problems. Françoise was not that lucky, but she is maintaining the upper hand, and she has a good attitude. Otherwise, we get up every morning, put one foot in front of the other, and enjoy each other's company. Aside of being married, we are also the best of friends, and companions, and consider ourselves very fortunate. There are millions of people, who would like to walk in our shoes today (although not in mine, during the Holocaust). It is reassuring to know that my best Friend, God, is watching over us.

January, February, March and April go by very quickly, as we attend all the lectures we have scheduled. We have received hundreds of letters from students and educators, and we have a system for reading each letter. Some are very well composed, reflecting the maturity of the students. Those we place in a protective plastic cover, and we save them in a binder. The others we keep in large plastic containers, up in the attic. It takes up lots of space, and time, to keep them organized.

Invitation to Dachau and My Former Campsite Muhldorf on the 70th Year after Liberation

On April 21st, I received a phone call from Munich, Germany. A reporter, Gregory Schiegel, from the *South Deutsche Zeitung* interviewed me for over a half hour, and asked me permission to print the interview. In 2015, I got an invitation from the German government, offering to cover all of our expenses, and fly us to Dachau, a former Concentration Camp, in Germany. I was informed that German Chancellor Dr. Angela Merkel, would be the keynote speaker on May 3rd.

Our good friend Elfie, a professor in German, French, and English, asked if she could join us on our trip. Elfie has traveled with us on several Holocaust related trips. She was born and raised in Germany, and she is writing about the German Resistance during World War II. While researching the book, she travels frequently back to her birth place. She volunteered and prepared our entire travel itinerary, including nonstop flights from Las Vegas to Frankfurt and Munich.

The rest of the program was set up by the German authorities. We left on April 28th, arrived in Frankfurt, and took the connecting flight to Munich. After collecting our luggage, and passing through customs, we were happy to see someone holding up a sign, "Nasser". We were transported to our hotel in Dachau. On the following day, Elfie bought the Munich paper, *South Deutsche Zeitung*, and showed us excitedly the quarter page article with my picture in it. Shortly after, we were bussed to Kaufering, a World War II underground airplane factory and Concentration Camp. We attended ceremonies and speeches, and then we all had lunch and returned to the hotel.

Previously, we had made arrangements to meet with our good friends, Heinz, (in 2010, he had translated **My Brother's Voice** into the German edition, **Die Stimme meines Bruthers**) and Milena, and Wolfgang (in 2012 they were the ones who made it possible to have the Stolpersteins installed in front of the "Nasser House" in Budapest). We were joined by Walter, the filmmaker, and his son, Daniel (in 2011 he had introduced me to the German public, while presenting his documentary film, *End Station Seeshaup* and my book, **Stimme meines Bruders**).

Walter and Daniel picked us up from our hotel on April 30th, around 3:00 P.M. I was invited by Seeshaupt Burgermeister, # 1, Michael Bernwieser to dedicate a large, memorial bronze plaque commemorating the 70th year of the liberation of the "Death Train" back on April 30th, 1945, from Muhldorf Concentration Camp. At the same place, 70 years ago we were pulled out from under dead bodies by General Patton's III Army.

We were running late, but thanks to Walter's expert driving, we arrived just in time at Seeshaupt Railroad Station. There was a large crowd waiting for us at the memorial ceremony; there was the Burgermeister, Peter Weishoff, Walter, and Daniel, and in colorful Bavarian attire, a gentleman playing local tunes on his harmonica. I spoke for about five minutes, with the translation done by Daniel.

fter the ceremony, Françoise, Elfie, and I were driven about a half mile away in the village to a Memorial which had been dedicated back in 1995 to the prisoners who perished on the "Death Train." The road was closed to traffic and benches and chairs were placed in front of the metal sculpture. After people walked over from the Station, there was standing room only. At the

70 th. year of Liberation from the Death Train

Seeshaupt railroad station, Memorial plaque, 2015.

conclusion of this second commemoration, the Burgermeister had a dinner reception for a handful of us in a nearby restaurant. Poor Walter must have had a long day, after he drove Françoise, Elfie, and I back to the hotel in Dachau, about 50 miles away.

The following day we had to rise early, as a bus picked us up and drove us to Muhldorf, the site of the former Concentration Camp, where I was also a prisoner. Sad memories! Seventy years ago, I lost my beloved brother, Andris when he died in my arms. The Camp's work area was deep in the forest, and the Burgermeister of Muhldorf drove us along the muddy road. Below the remains of the towering cement arches, were a couple of hundred chairs set up, for the attendees of the commemoration. We were at the mercy of the weather, and were lucky to escape the rain with none of us getting wet. There were several dignitaries speaking, a few survivors and I followed them at the improvised podium.

Pista under the cement arch he was forced to build as a prisoner, Muhldorf, Germany.

Stephen, Elfie ans Francoise.
Dachau Castle, 2015.

I expressed my feelings, remembering our lost family members.

Just as we were leaving the ruins, this older woman approached me, "Are you Stephen "Pista" Nasser?"

I gave her a positive answer.

She continued, "I don't suppose you remember me? My name is Marta."

As if lightning had struck me, without hesitation, I embraced her. "Marta, how could I ever forget you?" I exclaimed! "We youngsters came out together from Hungary in 1948!" (We came across on the ocean liner, *Aquitania* and landed in Halifax, Canada.)

Heinz Bickert arrived on the following day and joined us. He had recently become a new grandfather, as his daughter Sabrina, blessed them with a healthy granddaughter, Marieke. Heinz stayed with us for the rest of our stay in Bavaria. Later that evening, we all attended a reception at Dachau's Castle.

Marta introduced me to her grand-daughter, who looked very similar to her grandmother, 67 years ago.

On May 3rd, Elfie, Heinz, Françoise, and I were picked up from our hotel and taken to Dachau Concentration Camp. It was a rainy day, but we gathered in a huge tent, totally weather-proofed and air-conditioned. Elfie and Heinz found seating several rows behind us. Françoise and I had reserved seats in the second row. There were some Holocaust survivors present, but our number is shrinking rapidly, year after year. Besides us, there were over a thousand invited guests and dignitaries in attendance. The keynote speaker was Chancellor Dr. Angela Merkel, who was introduced by Karl Feller. Mr. Feller, during his introduction, mentioned the importance of my book, *Stimme meines Bruders* being read in the schools.

I decided to sign a book for the Chancellor, personalize it, and hand it to her if security would allow me to do so.

Before the ceremony started, I approached a couple of security people and identified myself. They assured me that after the Chancellor left the podium, they would allow me to hand her my book. It took some maneuvering. She was very gracious, and thanked me

Francoise and Stephen before presenting book to Chancellor Dr. Angela Merkel of Germany.

and shook my hands, with a parting pat on my shoulder.

On May 4th, we said goodbye to Elfie, as she had to return to Las Vegas to her college. Heinz drove us to Herrsching by the Ammersees. We checked into Hotel Garni, our cozy Gasthause, which had a small porch overlooking the lake. Every morning we had breakfast, weather

German Chancellor Dr. Angela Merkel,
in Dachau.received Stephen's Book, 2015.

permitting, eating on the terrace overlooking the lake. Heinz had a similar room. Françoise and I were there because of the previous arrangements made by Milena, Wolfgang, and Heinz. We had planned to fly back early with Elfie, but after our three friends insisted on us having a small vacation, we gave in. They promised to visit and stay with us at a future date in Las Vegas. The same evening, we were invited to Milena's place for cake and coffee. We had a great reunion, and the conversation carried on for hours. The following day Heinz drove all of us around the lovely countryside. They understood that they would be our invited guests, for future meals. I had some resistance, but finally they agreed. We stopped by and ate in charming restaurants and all of us had a good time.

On May 7th, we had arranged to meet Walter and his wife, Kia in Tutzing at the Kurtheater. Walter's documentary film, *Endstation Seeshaupt*, was showing. Walter asked me to speak to the audience before the presentation, and to read a passage from my English version of **My Brother's Voice**. Following me, his wife, Kia read the same passage from the German version, **Die Stimme meines Bruders**. The audience was highly receptive. After our reading, the film started and ran for ninety minutes. Milena and Wolfgang watched the documentary, and Kia, Walter, Heinz, Françoise, and I went to a pizza place, timing ourselves to be back at the theater in time for book signing, when the show ended. About 30% of the audience purchased the book, and I personalized each one. We conversed outside the theater, and said a warm good- bye to Kia and Walter. They drove back to Seeshaupt, and

Milena, Wolfgang, Heinz, Françoise, and I returned to Herrsching. We had had one busy day!

One afternoon we drove up to Kloster Andechs, located on a lovely hillside, and parked the car at the parking area below. Françoise and I had to make it up the slopes very slowly. Milena also has difficulty walking. By the time we got up to the large terrace of the Monastery, we were ready to sit down, enjoy the view, and satisfy our appetites. Heinz and I toasted with two mugs of frosty Bavarian beer. Françoise and I thoroughly enjoyed the "Schwein Huck" (pig knuckles, the best in Bavaria). We all had a fantastic time and we returned to our hotel.

The following day was our last night together. Milena and Wolfgang choose one of his favorite restaurants overlooking the lake, and we finished up our dinner with an aromatic cappuccino.

On May 10th, our vacation came to an end and Milena and Wolfgang drove to our hotel. We took pictures and bid each other a warm good-bye. It was heartwarming to be able to spend several good days in the company of good friends. Heinz drove us to Munich, and we all checked into a hotel, not far from the airport. Talk about friends? They had spoiled us rotten! Heinz insisted and accompanied us as we boarded our flight to Frankfurt and then nonstop to Las Vegas on Condor Airlines. We said an affectionate good-bye to our good friend Heinz.

Heinz, Milena, Francoise, Stephen and Wolfgang, Celebrating Bavarian style, 2015.

Back in Las Vegas, Leigh, our longtime friend, picked us up, and we got home to rest up from jetlag, and the exciting, but emotional experiences of the past twelve days. We could not have too much rest, as we had to set our alarm to wake us up at 5:30 A.M.

We had a lecture scheduled at Seville Middle School starting at 7:30 A.M. As usual, we had to get there a half hour before, to set up my power point. For the past several years we have been invited by Lawrence, a good teacher and friend. He has a special arrangement with us, and at 7:30 A.M., we were joined for breakfast with about 50 students. They purchased breakfast and a T-shirt from the school, so they could eat with us. After breakfast we had lots of questions to answer. After eating, the students formed a line, and I was handed a white marking pen. I signed the back of each student's shirt, one by one. Several years ago they started this custom, and at that time Françoise and I were each given a couple of maroon shirts. On the back says, "11 Million", and on the front ""*Never Again*", Stephen Nasser Holocaust Survivor". Wherever we speak, we both wear this T shirt (Faiss High School in Las Vegas, started these T shirts many years ago, with a similar logo). After breakfast we went to the gym which was all set up for 400 students to assemble. They listened for over an hour, while watching my power point presentation, followed by book signing.

In May, I received a very nice thank-you letter from Germany from the "Buro der Bundeskanzlerin", Dr. Angela Merkel, the Chancellor of Germany, expressing her thanks for the book I signed and handed to her in Dachau, on May 3rd. She said, "After reading it, it will stay in my private library."

In June I got a phone call from Austria. Teresa Arrieta, from *Purkarthofer-PR.*, requested an interview on Skype, about my Holocaust experience, regarding *My Brother's Voice* and *Die Stimme meines Bruders*. On June 6th, she Skyped me and the interview lasted just over an hour.

Since we returned from Germany, we have had five more speaking engagements, although they have started to slow down, because school is out for the summer. Finally we could relax. This time of the year, Spring Mountain State Park, starts its theater program. For years we have enjoyed spending an evening out with the Ann and Leigh at this lovely location. We picked them up and drove to our favorite Summer Theater. It is an unusual place, set in a grassy meadow under the shadow of tall rocky peaks.

Andris's Memorial Plaque, Spring Mountain, Nevada.

From the parking lot through the scrubby desert landscape there is a walk-way winding down to the amphitheater. It is paved by flagstones. These stones display the engraved names of people immortalized, by someone who

Michele's Memorial Plaque, Spring Mountain, Nevada.

cared. I made sure that my daughter Michele and my brother Andris were represented on this walk of memory.

This time we had company joining us, Ann's brother, David and his wife, Joy. They are visiting from China, and their son, Chris lives with his aunt and uncle while he is getting his education here in Nevada. Our conversation concentrated around the stage. David remarked, turning to Ann and I, "I can visualize your play, *Not Yet, Pista* to be staged here, playing to a houseful of an audience!"

Ann gave me a wink and said, "Stephen and I worked hard for over a year, and finally the script is finished."

I replied, "Nothing can stop us, after we raise the necessary funds!"

We had a good laugh, as Ann clowned around, singing, "Money makes the world go around.........", and we all joined in. People looked at us, but we didn't pay them any attention. We were all in great spirits.

The stage darkened, and spotlights lit up as the actors and the sound of music opened the play. Two hours later, when it was over, in the now-darkened desert, we got back into our car. We followed the brake lights of the long line of cars, heading towards the highway, from the dirt road. We had our windows rolled down, to let in some fresh night air. Besides the noise of slowly moving cars, we clearly heard some wild mules greeting each other.

While driving home, some of my passengers had their eyes closed. I had time to thank God for the opportunity, to grant me a chance to travel so far in my Journey to Freedom. High above was the moon and I felt the presence of my beloved brother. If I could hear his voice, he would say, *"My Little Brat, I'm so proud of you, you still have time enjoy, it is too early to join me, Not Yet, Pista!"*

Disclosure

Ever since I lost any connection with Vera, several establishments, including the Mormon Temple in Salt Lake City, have offered to help locate her. During all of these years I have just wanted to know if Vera was all right. Each time we visited Budapest, Françoise encouraged me to look for Vera. One organization known as Allgeneration is headed by Serena Woolrich. We had met her in Washington D.C. She is a great and highly motivated person. Her services reach countless people across the globe, who have been involved with the Holocaust. She has tried several times to find Vera. A couple of years ago, Serena got information about Vera's brother Attila, who was a chess master, but unfortunately he had passed away in 1997. The trail of information got cold until July 21st, 2015.

We were at home in Las Vegas, when I received a phone call from Serena. "Mr. Nasser, I've gotten an email from Hungary. A person unknown to me has written that he knew of the Koranyis (Vera's family). The parents died and Attila's widow is still alive, and through her we got information that Martha, Attila's sister, lives in Budapest with her husband and son." She paused and I detected a hesitation.

Then I asked her excitedly, "What about Vera? Is she all right?"

I felt like minutes passed before she replied, "I'm so sorry to inform you that Vera passed away five years ago."

I was shocked. For sixty-seven years I had hoped to hear about her well-being and now that uncertainty has vanished. I was deeply saddened. I knew the respect for our childhood romance was locked in my memory.

Vera in 1948 said good'bye to Pista.

Nobody could take that away from me. But the fact remained, she was gone forever.

In August 2015, I got an email from Budapest, Hungary from Vera's sister and her husband. Two days later their son Peter, an English teacher from Budapest, sent me a picture of young Vera!

It depicted her exactly the way she had remained in my memory all this time, when I said my good'byes to her way back in 1948.

Epilogue

Thank you for letting me take you on my life's journey. In 1948 when I left Hungary, I was 16 years of age and had youth on my side. I was determined to bring Vera to the free world and start a new life of our own, and to keep my promise to my brother. As I'm closing in on the end of my journey, the calendar has reached 2015. I'm 84 years old, with a lifetime of experiences behind me. I've learned some "Golden Rules" and would like to share them with you:

- What happened a second ago is History, no one can change it.
- Be proud of your heritage, wherever you were born.
- You are not responsible for the choices of others.
- Have respect for yourself, before others can respect you.
- Your future is in your hands, make responsible decisions.
- Turn your problems into challenges.
- You will achieve your goals by doing, not trying.
- During your lifetime you will have many acquaintances, but only a few friends.
- Life does not owe you a living, you have to earn it.
- Life is very simple, but people make it difficult.
- Live and let live.

I wish you all a long and happy life!
Stephen "Pista" Nasser

Acknowledgements

During my life I've met thousands of individuals. Most of these people have enriched our lives. There are not enough pages in this book to mention every single person whom I've met and to whom I am grateful for their friendship.

My best friend is Françoise, my wife. We have been married over 35 wonderful years. She is my soul mate and has stood beside me through good and difficult times. We have cheerfully walked through life, but we have shared some sad moments, too. Françoise made it possible to keep my lifetime commitment to my brother Andris wherever I was speaking worldwide.

We have been invited to share my story with the public since 1997, nationally and internationally. My first book, *My Brother's Voice* was published in 2003.

Our travels have involved many thousands of miles, driving to several states, to fulfill our speaking engagements. When we were in California, my daughter Michele and her husband Paul welcomed us every time, as we stayed with them during our lecture tours. Since Michele's tragic death, Paul and June (his new wife) receive us annually with open arms in their home.

Special recognition goes to my granddaughter Chelsea Lauren Jones, who with her artistic talent designed the front cover of my German book, *Die Stimme meines Bruders* and the cover of this book, *Journey to*

Freedom. She is a recognized photographer who resides in Hollywood. Whenever we are at her father's house in Chino Hills, she makes sure to spend some time with us. June and Paul Jones and Chelsea usually spend Thanksgiving at our home in Las Vegas.

On our California circuit, we have been invited on several occasions to Townsend Junior High, Chino High School, Magnolia Junior High School, Ramona Junior High School, and Upland Public Library. In Covina, we have invitations from Sierra Vista Middle School, in Ontario, Woodcrest Junior High School and Chaffey High School, and in Cerritos Valley, Christian Middle School. In the San Francisco area, my second cousin, Carol and Mike Kulakofsky, have welcomed us for several days and arranged many speaking engagements in neighboring schools. While in Arizona, we have our good friends Barbara and Mike Burch in Sedona, Pat and Ray Newton in Prescott, and Diana and Scot Gordon in Glendale, who always greet us with open arms. Lee Vore and his wife Marilyn have hosted us on several occasions. In St. George, Utah live our good friends Susie and Chuck Andrews who have warmly welcomed us every time we stayed with them. These individuals have introduced us to their immediate families and they have made us feel like we were at home. We spent time with good memories at the home of Corinne and Peter Cevaer and family in Santa Barbara while speaking at Thatcher School.

I also would like to mention the countless number of teachers, schools, libraries, synagogues, churches, and institutions, who all helped me to deliver my message through so many years. We are so thankful to all of them.

Yes, we have driven many thousands of miles, and sometimes extended days, to keep up with our busy schedules. Neither of us is getting any younger; to the contrary, age is catching up with both of us. But we have our best Friend looking after us and of course I want to keep the promise I gave to my brother for as long as I can. God bless you all who made my Journey to Freedom a success.

Stephen "Pista" Nasser

Made in the USA
San Bernardino, CA
19 March 2019